Billie B. Daniel (signature)

Sweetheart of the Carolinas

The Youngest

Of the Blues Singers

Billie Burton Daniel

Sweetheart of the Carolinas

ISBN-13: 978-0-9792039-4-7

ISBN-10: 0-9792039-4-5

CatPav Publishing

Fayetteville, NC 28303

www.catpavpublishing.com

Foreword

In the beginning, I write this as a child, and I tell it as a child, for that is the way I remember it. If by chance, and certainly very possibly, my childhood bores you, then I ask that you skip to page 51, for this is where I begin to grow up and where it may prove to be more interesting.

I started in my childhood, because I believe that the people who colored my life are responsible for the way I am. I believe as well, that heredity plays the biggest part in who we are. As you can tell, I revere my family and am very proud of my heritage. I seek neither fame nor fortune, for I am cognizant of the fact that the things that matter most in this life are the things that money cannot buy. I am content, with who I am, and I have never wanted to be anybody else. Certainly, I have made many, many mistakes, and certainly, I have many regrets. I have accepted the fact that I can do nothing about them, so in these my latter years, I try not to dwell on disappointments that have come my way, and I have endured many, but I am thankful for the blessings and the happiness that I have known.

Never a minute goes by that I don't miss my child, my daughter, my life, Jennie; that I don't wish her life could have been happier, that her life could have been more complete. Maybe there was a reason that God took her when she was still relatively so young. Maybe there was a reason for the disappointments that were hers, disappointments that she couldn't face without the most lethal, the most insidious drug of all, alcohol. Maybe God took her to keep her away from this evil crutch on which she leaned. I can only hope that she is happy now, that she goes on in a better world, and I look forward to the time when I can join her, to the time when once again I'll be re-united with the people I love, for most of the ones that I hold dearest are now in that wonderful, that miraculous place, God's heaven.

So, if you find the time, read my book. They say that every life is a story, this then is my story. You just may find it interesting.

Table of Contents

It very simply seems to me

The saddest thing of all to be

Is what I am

Oh, God, why did you make of me

This thing I prayed I'd never be

Her survivor

Billie Burton Daniel

We Moved to Littleton ♫

We moved to Littleton when I was six and my sister, King King, was four and a half. We had visited in Littleton many times because that was Mama's home. She'd been born there and she had two whole brothers and two half brothers and one half sister there. Now, that's what she told me, but I'll tell you they looked whole to me. Can you imagine a half of a person? Well, I cannot. That would mean they just had one arm and one leg, wouldn't it? Then, please tell me how in the world they could walk. Well, though, I do, on Daddy's side have an uncle in law who just has one leg, but that's because he had one cut off by a train, but he has two eyes and two arms, so you certainly can't call him half of a person, can you? Now, what do you think?

I am very smart, you know. One Sunday morning when I was four years old, and we were still living in Wilmington, King King and I got in bed with Mama, cause Daddy had gotten up early, and the paper hadn't come, and so he had gone down town to get one, and besides we liked to get in bed with Mama 'cause she would tell us stories about when she was a little girl and lived out on her papa's farm, before her mama made him build a house in Littleton so she would be nearer her own Mama and Papa and all her sisters and brother. My Grandmamma Willie just had one brother, and he was as wild as a buck. He had gone to school way up in New York at Columbia and had turned into some sort of wild man. I have never seen him, but I do look forward to meeting him some day. My daddy started drinking when he was going to school in Chapel Hill. I have made up my mind not to ever go away to school, that is, unless they build back Littleton Female College that used to be here in Littleton, before it burned down, 'cause that is where Grandmamma Willie and all seven of her sisters went, and even my mama went to high school there, and none of them went wild.

Anyway, to get on with my story about how smart I am, this Sunday morning Mama was talking about her little brother, Gideon. She thought he was the handsomest of boys, and she could not believe that he was fifteen years old now and would soon be a grown man, so I just started counting up on my fingers, and I said, "Well, that means Gideon is eleven years older than I am." Well, you would have thought I had set the house on fire! Daddy was coming in the front door with his paper, and Mama said, I mean, she hollered, "Bennie, come here, Willie is a genius." Well, Daddy was almost as excited as she was, and he said, "Tom," that's what he called me. "Tom, how did you figure that out, are you sure you never heard Mama say that Gideon was eleven years your senior?", and I said, "No sir," and I told him how I counted it up. So Daddy said, right then and there, "Fannie Kingsland, we have really got to start thinking about a good school for Willie," and I started crying, and I said, "Please, no sir, I don't want to be a wild woman." Well, Daddy just laughed, and he assured me that young ladies never went to schools that turned them into wild women.

Well, I still wasn't sure that I wanted to go away to college, but Mama said not to worry, that it would be a long, long time before I had to be concerned about that. I thought, though, that I needed to practice my number work anyway, and I found the perfect office for me underneath the table in the kitchen; it was sort of private under there what with the table cloth and all. So I would go under the table and be as quiet as a mouse, and sometimes Annie Newkirk, our cook, wouldn't even know I was under there.

I made a startling discovery while I was practicing my number work one day. That was where Annie Newkirk hid her snuff. I had never, until that time, tasted snuff, but you must admit it smells pretty good. So, because after all I was a genius, and I was big enough to have my own office, I decided to put some in my lip like she did; so I pulled out my bottom lip, and I poured in the snuff and I have never to this day, been so sick!!!!

I really thought my time had come right then. Annie Newkirk screamed for Mama, and Mama came and held a cold wash cloth to my face, and I upchucked and upchucked and thought I never was gonna stop.

Mama called Dr. Crouch and told him what had happened, and he told her just to put me to bed when I stopped being sick, and I would be fine. So she rocked me to sleep, and I didn't eat any supper that night, and then the next day I felt pretty good. And do you know what my Daddy did? Just when I was beginning to feel like a human being, and even before he went to work, he told me to run out doors and break off a switch and bring it to him. Well, right then and there, I knew what was coming, and to this day I don't know why, as smart as I was, I didn't know that the little switches hurt more than the big ones. Anyway, as was his favorite expression, he wore me out, and then he went to work. And Mama had to rock me to sleep again right in the middle of the morning, and I didn't even do my number work that day. My Daddy was very hard to understand sometimes.

I started off telling about when we moved to Littleton, but have you ever noticed that when you tell one thing it makes you think of something else, and I just got to thinking about

4

how it was before we moved to Littleton when we lived in Wilmington.

My Grandpapa Amos Burton and my grandmamma Matt lived there too, and every Sunday morning Grandpapa came over with a big basket of fruit and nuts and a little bit of candy, too. We loved our Grandpapa very much, but then he went to heaven. I remember it very well, because we spent the night over at his house the night before 'cause he was sick with 'new monia.' Well, he refused to go to the hospital, and the doctor came over and sat with him. The doctor said it looked like the end was near, but he did think a good, strong drink of whiskey would probably help him as much as anything. They didn't have ABC stores then, I mean you couldn't just go to the store and buy whiskey, even if you did need it because of pro-a-bation. Anyway, Daddy said he knew where he could find some, and Mama said she bet he did. Mama hated whiskey. And so he went to get it, and he stayed and he stayed, and when he finally did get home he had been drinking and then all hell broke loose. That's what I heard him tell Uncle Edwin the next day.

Uncle Edwin had come all the way from Texas, because Grandpapa was sick, and then Grandpapa left almost immediately for heaven. Anyway, that very night Grandpapa

5

moved to heaven, I don't know how he got there, but when I got up the next morning I saw these men taking this long thing down the steps. It was all covered up with a sheet, and about that time Mama came running out in the hall and made me go back in the bedroom. I asked her where was Grandpapa, 'cause he wasn't in his room, and she told me that he had gone to heaven, and I am still wondering how he got there, and why in the world did they have to cover him up with a sheet to get him there. There are a few things I do not understand, but Daddy says I will when the time comes.

Daddy said what really caused Grandpapa to leave this world was the stock market crash. Grandpapa was in real estate, and he lost everything, including the will to keep going. Well, Daddy lost everything, too, but thank goodness; he did not leave and go to heaven. What saved Daddy was that several years before Grandpa moved to heaven he and his guide were out in the woods hunting. His guide was an Indian and Grandpapa thought a lot of him. Something happened to this Indian, something bad, I don't know what. He may have been caught in a bear trap or something. Anyway Grandpapa saved his life, and do you know what that Indian did? He appreciated it so much; he gave Grandpapa the formula for a miracle medicine that he said would cure anything. Well, Grandpapa was a little skeptical, but he showed Daddy the formula, and I'm mighty

6

glad he did. So having nothing better to do, and plenty of time to do it, after the stock market crashed and Grandpapa moved to heaven, Daddy made some of the medicine and took it out in the country and sold it to some farmers, (My Daddy could sell anything.) Well, to his amazement, the farmers came looking for him. The medicine worked!!!! and that was the beginning of Burton's Relief. Business was so good that everybody wanted to get in on it, and that's when we moved to Littleton, cause two of Mama's uncles-in-law and her whole brother, Uncle William, went in business with him.

And so we moved to Littleton, and I want you to know that Mama cried every step of the way, 'cause she said she absolutely did not want to live in Cousin Sam Donald's old monstrosity, that she had always hated it, and it was gonna kill her to have to live there. Uncle William had sent three of his big trucks to move our furniture. (He had a big wholesale grocery company, and a whole bunch of big trucks.) They were right behind our car following us, because they didn't know the way back to Littleton. (I don't know how in the world they ever got to Wilmington in the first place if they couldn't find the way back.) King King and I and Trouble, our dog and Herbert Hoover, our cat, were in the back seat trying to sleep, 'cause they had gotten us up at the crack of dawn. Well, Mama just sat in the front seat fussing as hard as she could, and I will admit, she was probably the best fusser I have ever heard. Anyway, Daddy kept saying, "Fannie Kingsland, I do wish you would be quiet, you are going to cause me to have a wreck and kill these children, and then all those trucks behind us are going to run into us, and William will be mad as hell." Finally, Daddy got so mad, he just slammed on the brakes and stopped, and don't you know, you could hear all those trucks trying to stop and the brakes were screeching and they were going all over the road. Daddy just sat there and gathered his wits, and finally he spoke, in a very soft voice. (I had to strain real hard to hear him.) He said, "Now listen, Madam," that's what he called her when he was exasperated, he said, "I will build you a house to your liking just as soon as I can get somebody lined up to do it, but you can not build a house over night, and besides there is nothing at all wrong with Cousin Sam's house, in fact, its really a fine old place, and it was the only vacant house I could find. So now, you just pull yourself together, and you ought to be ashamed to let your children see you acting like a spoiled child." Well, I did not know what he meant by pulling herself together, cause she looked like she was all in one piece to me. I even sat up and looked in the front seat, and she certainly looked together. So we started off again, and Mama didn't say a word.

By this time though, King King and I had given up trying to sleep. We started playing paper dolls, and do you know what I did? I dropped my very favorite paper doll down on the inside of the car door. I was holding her up against the window, so she could see out side, when all of a sudden she just slipped right out of my hand and went down inside the door. Then I started screaming, and Daddy slammed on the brakes again cause he thought I had been mortally wounded, and he said, "What in the hell is wrong now" and Mama said, "Bennie Burton, don't you dare curse in front of my children". Well, by this time I was crying. I did not want that paper doll to fall out of the car door, and probably get run over by one of Uncle William's trucks. Daddy tried and tried to get that paper doll out of the door, but he never could. All three of the truck drivers came and tried to help, but they never could find it. To this day, I don't know where it went. Anyway, I cried so much I was finally overcome with sleep, and the next thing I knew we were in Littleton.

Littleton was, probably, the closest thing to heaven in this world. You cannot imagine how many aunts and uncles and great aunts and uncles and cousins we had, and most of them lived on Mosby Avenue, except my grandmother Willie, and my great aunt, Eliza, and that was because they were both dead; but they had. They all just loved King King and me to death, because there just were not that many children in the family.

King King and I didn't mind Cousin Sam's monstrosity at all. We had the biggest orchard you have ever seen way out in back with almost every kind of fruit tree you can imagine and great big fig trees; we couldn't wait for them to get ripe. And there were fresh asparagus growing out there and all kinds of herbs and spices. And that house was so big it had a lot of secret places, and we explored a lot; you'd be amazed at some of the things we found. One thing was an old ink well that Daddy said was probably two hundred years old and very valuable, because cousin Sam had a lot of artifacts that he'd collected all over the world. He told me to put it back where I found it, but I didn't. I gave it to Aunt Dollie, because she had a lot of old furniture, in fact she had a great big old rosewood desk that she said had been in our family over two hundred years, but she did not have a beautiful ink well like that, so I took it up to her house and gave it to her, and she really appreciated it. She asked me where on earth I had gotten it, and I just said I had found it, which in truth, is what I did. (I always tried to tell the truth, but some times it was kind of hard). Thank goodness, though, she kept the desk closed most of the time, so Daddy never did see it.

The best thing about living at Cousin Sam's, though, was that it was right next door to Aunt Ellen's, and that was the most fun place in the world. Aunt Ellen was always having company. All the Burton girls, who were the most beautiful and glamorous people in the world, except Mama, of course, came often. They were my great Aunt Eliza's children. (I've already explained to you that she was dead.) The oldest one, Frances Burton, taught elocution, and was in a lot of plays on Broadway in New York, and she was very dramatic. She really taught me a whole lot. That's why, at a very early age, I decided to be in show business. The other two, Edna and Elizabeth, were high fashion models, and were just absolutely beautiful. They always brought their riding habits, boots and everything with them, 'cause they loved to ride and go hiking in the woods, and sometimes they would let me go with them. Their boy friends were always coming to see them in Pierce Arrows and Rolls Royce's. We were just crazy about the Burton girls, and you cannot imagine the boxes of beautiful clothes they sent for us to wear when we played dress up.

The Burton girls had a brother, too. His name was James and he came often. We looked forward to his visits. He had a car with a rumble seat and he would take us to ride a lot.

One Sunday afternoon he took us for a ride way out in the country. We went everywhere. He would pull up in the driveway and blow his horn, and when the farmer came out he'd ask him if he had any 'corn', and when the farmer said "no" we'd go on to another farm. I tried to tell him that he didn't need to look for corn, because Wiggins Lee had a whole lot of it out in Aunt Dollie's garden. Wiggins Lee worked for Aunt Dollie. He tended the garden and polished the Ivy, and brought in the wood and made the fires.) Well, James didn't pay me one bit of attention, he just kept on searching. Finally one place we went had some. I figured he'd get at least a bushel of it since he had worked so hard to find it, but do you know what he got came in a bottle, and whatever it was it certainly wasn't corn. James got in a happy mood then, and he took us to Cousin 'Lijar Perry's drug store and brought us a Dixie Cup.

When we got home Mama and Daddy were worried to death, because we'd been gone so long, and I told them we'd just had a real hard time finding the kind of corn James was looking for, well then 'you know what' broke loose. Daddy got mad as fire with James and said we couldn't ever go to ride with him anymore. That just broke our hearts, cause we loved riding in James' rumble seat. I thought Daddy was gonna stay mad forever, but he didn't. After a while he let us go to ride with James again, but we never went looking for corn with him again. Sometimes James would let us ride on the running board; we really liked that, but then Daddy found out. Daddy didn't understand children at all.

Aunt Ellen and Uncle George had a daughter named Frances Vick, and she was the bossiest thing you have ever seen. She was determined to make us act like who we were, because we were Alstons and Kingslands and Daniels, and you could not get any better than that. We were blue bloods, she said, but I wasn't. I fell down and hurt my knee, really bad, and it bled, and that blood was as red as blood. I didn't tell Mama, because I certainly did not want her to know that she had a red blooded child, so I went in the bathroom and washed my own knee, and I put Mercurochrome all over it. I mean, I just poured it on, so she couldn't see what color my blood was, and I'll tell you the truth, I did spill some of it on the bathroom floor, but at least she didn't have to learn the truth about me, and I, frankly, don't think I deserved the switching I got when Daddy came home.

14

Aunt Ellen had a colored man and woman who worked for her, Anna and Norman, they were married and they had a little girl named Frances Vick too. They named her after my cousin. I was crazy about them. Norman worked mostly out doors, he milked the cow, which lived way, way out back behind the garages where the chickens lived, and he worked in the garden. I liked to go out there with him sometimes and help him pull weeds. I always made it my business to take a salt shaker with me, because he grew the best tomatoes I have ever tasted, and I will tell you, nothing is better that a warm tomato right off the vine.

They had a huge back yard, before you got to the garages, that had the best scuppernong grape vine that had the best grapes I have ever tasted, and they had a huge, gigantic rock garden and fish pool with gold fish that were as big as real fish. If you stuck your finger in the water they would swim up and kiss it. They also played Croquet a lot back there after supper in the summer time and that was, really, lots of fun, even Mama and Daddy enjoyed that. Norman would be turning the handle on the ice cream freezer, making the best peach ice cream you've ever tasted, and Anna would come out with a huge pitcher of lemonade. They also had a sandbox for us so we could build toad frog houses, and the next morning, rain or shine, we'd go out there, and sure enough, there would be

Hershey's silver bells inside. Norman drove for them, too, and when he did, he was all dressed up in livery. Daddy said he thought that was a little pretentious, but he was sure it was Frances Vick's doing. She had 'delusions' of grandeur, whatever that is. I don't think it was serious, though, and Daddy said it wasn't contagious. In some ways, when Frances Vick wasn't being bossy, she was the best thing in the world to us. On rainy days, when we couldn't go out and play, we would lie down with her, on her big brass bad, and she would read poetry to us from the book, 101 Poems. Maybe that's why poetry has been a very important part of my life. My favorite poem was Little Boy Blue by Eugene Field. That is one of the most beautiful poems I have ever heard.

Well, anyway, King King and I were very happy living at Cousin Sam's, but every morning, while we were having breakfast and Daddy had gone to work, Aunt Dollie would come. She lived just two doors on the other side of Aunt Ellen. She and her sister, Lil, lived in my great grandparent's home. Well, actually, it was their home then, because when my great grandmamma Fannie Kingsland and great Grandpapa Billy died, they left them the house, because they were still unmarried. (To tell you the truth, they always were.) Anyway, Aunt Dollie wanted us to move in with them, because they had plenty of room, and she was just afraid we would freeze to death in that big barn of a house. I don't think Cousin Sam or Cousin Lizzie ever froze, and they raised all three of their children there. Cousin Sam was a very good Judge, I understand, but, they say that Cousin Lizzie never was quite all there. That's another thing that puzzles me a lot.

So finally, Mama persuaded Daddy, and we all moved in with Aunt Dollie and Lil. Rosalie, our nurse, came with us too, and of course, Trouble and Herbert Hoover. Well, we just loved it, and Mama was happy again. We were crazy about Aunt Dollie. She was this great big woman, not fat really, just a big woman, a very 'stately' looking woman, Mama said. She stood as straight as an arrow, and always held her head up high. She was, probably, the best cook in the world. She always had a cook, but she did the cooking, and she could go out in the poultry yard and ring a chicken's neck just as easy as pie. I went with her a lot of the time, 'cause I liked to see it flop around. Now, I do not know why Wiggins Lee didn't kill the chickens. Mama said she had never been able to understand how Aunt Dollie could bring herself to do that. Every morning right after breakfast Aunt Dollie would go to the telephone and tell Central to connect her to Kenyon's Grocery Store. Then she'd order her groceries for the day. She never, as long as I can remember, ever went to the grocery store. Like I said before, she was probably the best cook in the world, and believe me if every single thing she ordered wasn't as fresh as she thought it should be, she'd send it straight back to the store.

Aunt Dollie could do just about anything she wanted to do though. She had a pistol, which she put on the mantelpiece in her bedroom every night. She would always go in the dining room and get General George Kingsland's silver teapot, too. George Kingsland was her great grandfather, and I'll tell you she was mighty proud of him, she would put the silver teapot on the mantelpiece right beside the pistol. That was hard for me to understand, and I asked her, "Why, if a robber sneaked in and got the teapot, wouldn't he see the pistol and take that, too?" Well, like I have said before, there are some things children do not understand, and that's what I was at the time.

Lil was a different story altogether. She was not very big at all, had the most beautiful feet I have ever seen and always wore high heels. I have always admired feet. Her hands were beautiful too. In fact, she was famous for her pretty figure and her style. Everything about Lil was small, except her nose, which was very aristocratic they said, but I still thought it was too big. I want you to know that we loved her very much, but she could be mean as a snake sometimes. She would not put up with any mess at all. I loved to go in the parlor and play the piano, I couldn't play anything but Chop Sticks and Jesus Loves

18

Me, but I played those a lot. Sometimes I would look through this huge stack of music, there must have been about a million pieces, and I never could get them back together exactly right, and boy, would she get mad! It was sort of unnerving to be in the parlor in the first place, because the walls were just covered with portraits of ancestors, and sometimes I would look up and they would all be staring a hole through me. There was one in particular that scared the hell out of me. (I never said that out loud so Daddy could hear me, but I thought it a lot.) We all thought she was the 'booger man'. At night when Daddy would send me downstairs to get him a drink of water, I was really scared to even go by that room, and I would always turn my head so I couldn't see Eliza Thayer. That's who she was, and she was my sixth great grandmother, but she was mean looking, and that's the truth.

But getting back to Lil, if there was one speck on the floor, I mean one tiny little speck, she would bend over and pick it up, and she would always blame me for tracking it in. The only thing she did all day was get the ice out for the tea. When I would hear that ice tinkling in the glasses I knew supper time was near. Well, I just remembered, she did do something else. Once a week, she would tie something around her head and she and Matilda would clean up. I mean they would move every stick of furniture in the house, not them, really, 'cause she wouldn't even let Matilda lift anything heavy, but she would call Wiggins Lee to come move it, and then he would have to come back in to move it back when they got through cleaning. I bet he didn't like that very much.

And this was another thing about Lil, there were these rolling doors between the reception hall and the back living room, the kind that didn't open, they just slid into the wall, and then you had to close them again. Now in the summer time it didn't matter cause they stayed open all the time, but in the winter, have mercy!!!! They had to be closed just as tight as a drum. Really and truly, it was just impossible for a child to do, but Lil did not take that into consideration. I'm telling you she fussed! She couldn't understand why we had to go in and out so much. She could be a pill, let me tell you.

Lil was really kind of funny, though. She would ask me to go to the bathroom for her, can you believe that? She would say, "Oh, darling, I have got to go to the bathroom so badly, would you be a good girl and go for me?" I would have done it, but I just didn't know how. I guess that's just something else I'll have to learn when the time comes.

I told you that Rosalie moved with us to Aunt Dollies'. Her room was not very far from ours, and we loved to go in her room at night and watch her 'stretch' her hair. That was most interesting. She had this comb made out of steel, and she had this old timey oil lamp like some people had who lived out in the country, where electricity didn't go. Well, she would put this thick, greasy stuff on her hair, (Her hair was really, really kinky) Then she would stick this steel comb down inside the lamp and hold it for a while 'til it got red hot. Then she would comb it through her hair, and you never heard so much sizzling and then her hair would be straight. It was just amazing.

We were crazy about Rosalie. Sometimes when she'd go home to see her family Mama would let us go with her. She had lots of little brothers and sisters, and we liked to play with them. Rosalie could tell the best ghost stories that scared the life out of us. Back then everybody knew lots of ghost stories. You see, television hadn't been invented then and there wasn't even a picture show in Littleton.

Sometimes we did things just to bedevil Lil. Like one time when my best friend Gertrude and I were upstairs playing, we thought it would be fun to tear up Daddy's paper in little bitty pieces and throw it over the banister just to see what Lil would do. Well, what she did was get mad as fire!!!!, and she came upstairs looking for me, and I had forgotten that when I was in my bedroom there was not any good way to get out when Lil was standing in the door. Of course, I could have jumped out the window, but I wasn't in the mood to do that, so the only thing I could think of was to get under the bed, which I did, but do you know, Lil moved that bed, and she didn't have to call Wiggins Lee to do it, either. Well, by this time I was beginning to get scared, so I started rolling to the other side of the bed, every time Lil was on the other side. Gertrude just ran out the door the first time Lil was moving the bed, and left me there to face her alone, and she was as much to blame as I was. Anyway, I just kept rolling from side to side, and finally Lil gave up and went downstairs, but just to be on the safe side, I decided to stay under the bed a while longer. When Daddy got home, I guess you know what happened.

Gertrude and I talked it over the next day, and decided to give Lil a party to make up for bedeviling her so much, so we did. We really did have a good party with all kinds of refreshments, we had bubble gum and Kool Aid, and some goose liver pate that was in the ice box, plus a great big tub of apples floating around in water but do you know, much as Lil appreciated that party, she never would bob for apples. I guess with her nose, she was afraid she might drown.

I forgot, when I said that all my great aunts lived on Mosby Ave., about one of my very dearest great aunts and the oldest one, Aunt Sallie. She and Uncle Will lived out in the country. We just loved to go out to see them. Uncle Will would saddle up one of his beautiful horses and let us ride. Uncle Will loved to go fox hunting, so he always had prize horses. We knew all the people who lived on their place and worked for them. Aunt Kibbee was their cook and had been with them for over 40 years.

Uncle Will used to come into town almost every morning early, and when we'd wake up we'd run out to the back porch to see what he'd left. In the summer time, there'd always be watermelons and cantaloupes and butter beans and corn and okra and tomatoes and every kind of vegetable you can imagine. Sometimes Uncle Will would ride his beautiful Palomino horse into town. We'd always run out to the street if we saw him coming, and he'd pull us up in the saddle with him. That was before they paved Mosby Ave.

As I told you before, we had about a million cousins, most of them were sort of old, but there were a few who were close to our age. Hattie Daniel and Sarah Piner Kenyon were the two we knew best. Hattie lived out in Airlie, which was about nine miles from Littleton. It was more fun than anything out there. Hattie's aunt Mary Long had a Hoover cart, which was the most fun thing in the world to ride. We would ride all through the woods and down country lanes and visit some of the colored people who lived on their farm. Sometimes, after supper at night, when we were sitting on the porch, these same people, would come and sing to us. They had the prettiest voices in the world. Mary Long would go in the house and bring them all a big glass of lemonade.

The other cousin was Sarah Piner Kenyon, who lived in Macon, which was ten miles from Littleton. She was on the Kingsland side of the family. Anyway, Sarah Piner's daddy had a great big grocery store in Littleton, so he came back and forth to Littleton everyday. His store stayed open real late on Saturday nights, so practically every Saturday, Harry Kenyon, who I do believe was aunt Dollie's favorite cousin, would come and have supper with us. King King just loved Harry to death, and he was crazy about her, too. Everybody thought she was so cute, because she was like a little butter ball and had naturally curly hair and every thing. I, personally, didn't have time to be cute. Anyway, on Saturday nights, King King would sit down in Aunt Dollie's favorite chair, which was the biggest chair in the back living room, and she wouldn't get up 'til Harry got there, so he could sit down and rest his tired bones. Well, naturally, that just tickled Harry to death, so he would take King King home with him lots of weekends so she could play with Sarah Piner.

Harry's wife was Lola, and I liked her a lot. Sometimes she would come and get both of us to spend the weekend. King King and Sarah Piner were inseparable, but I liked to stay in the den and discuss things with Lola. She and Julia, who was my Cousin Jimmy Jenkins's wife, could smoke more beautifully than any body I have ever seen. I decided on one of those weekends with Lola that I probably would smoke when I grew up. So right then and there I stopped biting my fingernails, because if you smoked you had to have beautiful hands. I had already been practicing a little bit.

This is the way it was, and this, too, was before we moved to Littleton. We were visiting Aunt Fannie this time. Her feelings would get hurt if we visited Aunt Dollie or Aunt Ellen more than her. We loved to visit her, too. Her cook was named Fannie, so everybody called her "colored Fannie", just purely and simply to distinguish between the two. They didn't have racism then; in fact, I don't think that word had been invented.

Anyway, Uncle Crowell, one of mama's half brothers, came to see us. We were just crazy about him. Well, he took out his cigarettes and put one in his mouth, and was about to light up when he said, "Oh! Excuse me girls, would you like a cigarette?" It was the first one I'd ever been offered so I took it, and then King King took one, and Mama was laughing, 'cause she thought it was funny, and then, Aunt Fannie came in. She did not think it was funny one bit, and she really fussed with Mama and told her that she should never, under any circumstances, laugh when her children were doing something that they should, most positively, not be doing, and she even fussed with Uncle Crowell. From then on, let me tell you, we never smoked anything, even rabbit tobacco when grown ups were around, and they nearly all the time were.

Aunt Fannie had this huge, gigantic rock way behind her house, It was sort of in the woods and all around it, growing every where, were the most delicious big, black grapes. I don't know to this day what kind of grapes they were, and I've never seen any anywhere, except there, but I will tell you they made your mouth itch something awful. Well, we decided that rock was about the most private place in the world, so we would go out there to do our smoking, which we did mostly when Sarah Piner came to see us, because she would ask her mother to take her by her daddy's store so she could bring us some candy and when nobody was looking she would also get a bag of Golden Grain cigarette tobacco, which her Daddy's store sold. We honestly felt we needed to keep in practice so we would smoke beautifully when we got grown. Aunt Fannie told Mama that Sarah Piner must really love grapes, cause every time she came we children spent a lot of time at the big rock. To tell you the truth, we were not always smoking while we were in the woods. We heard that you found babies under rocks, so we spent a lot of time looking under rocks. Mama told me that the stork brought babies, but I didn't believe that, because I never did even see a stork in Littleton, and a lot of people had babies.

Another thing we did was make money. Down town at the Chevrolet place, they had all these little pamphlets stacked up on a table with a sign that said, 'take one.' Which we did, in fact, we took a whole lot of them. Then we would take them around to all our kin people and sell them for a penny, you'd be surprised what a penny would buy, a BB-Bat or a little Hershey Bar or a stick of chewing gum, all kinds of candy. Cousin Tom Alston was our best customer.

Cousin Tom had a big peach orchard in his back yard, and he always said, "Go out in the orchard, children, and take a peach, take one home to your Mama, too." Well, we did, and Mama said, without a doubt, that was the best peach she had ever tasted. So, the next day we decided to go back and get some more of them. We stuffed them down inside our sun suits, 'cause we had forgotten to take a bag, besides we didn't want Cousin Tom to know we had gone into the peach business with his peaches. We took them around and sold them for a penny a piece.

Well, that night I started itching like fire from all that peach fuzz and Rosalie told Mama she thought King King and I both had the measles cause we had broken out with a rash. Well, to keep Daddy from calling Dr. Justus, which he was about to do, I just confessed and told him about our peach business.

I'm telling you, there really was 'you know what' to pay when Daddy found out what we had been doing. (I don't like to say curse words, but sometimes you just have to.) He marched me right back over to Cousin Tom's and made me tell him what we had done, me, just because I was the oldest, I got blamed for everything. Well, Cousin Tom didn't care; he said he had so many he didn't know what to do with them, anyway. Cousin Tom was a very nice man, and seemed to understand children much better than my Daddy did. I was hoping against hope that Daddy would forget that I needed a switching, but he didn't.

Another thing we did was pick blackberries, they grew everywhere in Littleton. Picking blackberries is hard work, because they get ripe in the very hottest part of the summer, and on top of that, you might get bitten by a snake, 'cause it's been said that wherever you see a blackberry, a snake is not very far away. Anyway, Aunt Dollie was always happy as a lark to buy them from us, and then we would have blackberry dumplings for supper.

Well, she'd pay us for the blackberries, a whole quarter, and then she would always put them on the back porch 'til after her nap. One day though, she was still asleep when we got up from our nap, and then I remembered that Aunt Ellen had said that she would be more than happy to buy some blackberries from us, and everybody knows two quarters are better than one, so I just decided to sell those on the back porch to her, and I did. I guess you know the consequences I suffered for that, and this time Aunt Dollie was on Daddy's side.

Frances Vick would pay us a whole quarter if we didn't end a sentence with a preposition for a week. That was kinda hard to do, but we did it; then if we were low on money, we would start asking, where's it 'at,' or what's it 'for', and we would start another week. That was good for a long time.

Another thing, which applied to only me, was if I would go for a whole week and call King King, Kingsland, I would get another dime. You see, when she was born, I was only one and a half years old, and I could not say Kingsland, and then everybody started calling her King King, and, of course I got blamed for that, too.

We had never had a lemonade stand, and Gertrude and I discussed it and decided to have one. I told Gertrude I would furnish the water and the tub if she would furnish the lemons and the sugar. Aunt Dollie said we could make the lemonade in the kitchen, if we didn't make a mess, 'cause Matilda had just scrubbed the floor. Well, Gertrude kept putting more and more sugar in it, and I told her that my Daddy wouldn't drink it if it was too sweet. Well, she said it was her sugar, and she wouldn't drink it if it was not sweet. I am telling you, I got so mad I had the strength of Sampson, and I just turned that great big tub over, and you never saw so much lemonade on a kitchen floor.

Aunt Dollie never did forget that, to her dying day, and Daddy gave me one of the worst switching I ever got, and Gertrude got so mad, she didn't come back to see me for a week.

My favorite money making scheme was having plays. I was the producer and always the star because I could sing. Well, we would rehearse and rehearse for days on end, and then when everybody knew their part I would go downtown to Uncle William's wholesale house and Mr. Stokes, who worked for Uncle William, would go with me to some far off part of the warehouse where they kept the crepe paper, and let me have all I wanted, and then we would prevail on Mama and Aunt Dollie and Aunt Ellen to make us some costumes. Then we would sell tickets to everybody in the family, and I must say they seemed to enjoy it very much. We had a perfect stage. Aunt Dollie had a six car garage way out in the back, it used to be a carriage house back in the days when people had horses and carriages and wagons. Uncle William paid Aunt Dollie to let him park some of his big trucks out there, so we thought the back of one of those trucks was a perfect place to have our shows. Everybody in the family would come and sit on folding chairs out in the yard to watch our plays.

Uncle William really was nice to us. Sometimes he'd get one of his truck drivers to fill up the bed of one of those trucks with hay, and then we'd have a hay ride. It would always end up out at Panacea Springs and we'd have a wiener roast and there were always lots of marsh mellows and watermelons too.

We loved the summer time. We looked forward all winter to going barefooted. Mama was all in favor of our going barefooted too; she thought maybe it would make our feet get wider. Her mama never would let her, and she blamed her narrow feet on that. It didn't work though. Anyway, I'm glad she thought it would. Norman (the one who worked for Aunt Ellen and Uncle George) saw us up town one day with Rosalie, and we didn't have any shoes on. Well, he made us get in the car with him, and he took us back home, and he really did fuss with Mama. Norman used to work for Grandpapa Bob a long time ago when he was still alive, and he had known Mama since she was little girl. He was really mad. He said "Miss Fannie Kingsland, I can't believe you let Mr. Bob Alston's grandchildren run around with no shoes on.

Your Papa is probably turning over in his grave right now. All the colored people in Littleton loved my Grandpapa Bob. They loved Mama too, and they thought she was the prettiest thing in the world.

After supper in the summertime, if we weren't up at Aunt Ellen's playing croquet, all the grown folks would sit on the front porch at night. I can still hear the hum of their voices and their laughter. We were all just so happy then. (Except the time a bat flew up on the porch, and they were all screaming and carrying like you wouldn't believe. Aunt Dolly, as big as she was climbed up on a chair and pulled her dress up over her head. They all did.) King King and I were usually out in the yard catching lightning bugs. If Gertrude and Mary Ellen or some of our little cousins were there we'd play "Red Light" or "May I?" We just always had so much fun. When it really got dark though (and we were having the best time in the world)

32

Daddy would make us come in, then he'd call upstairs and tell Rosalie it was time to put us to bed.

In the wintertime Mama and Rosalie would both put us to bed. After our baths they'd hold blankets up close to the stove and when they were warm as toast they'd wrap us up in those blankets and it was almost like being in heaven.

Catastrophes ♫

We had several catastrophes while we lived at Aunt Dolly's. One that sticks in my mind was the Christmas Eve that we thought we had lost Lil. It was this way.

The weather could not have been worse, I, frankly, was worried that Santa Clause might not be able to even get there. It was raining and snowing and sleeting all at the same time, and that rain was freezing as soon as it hit the ground. On top of that, the wind was blowing about 90 miles an hour.

Well, Lil was determined to go to the cemetery to put flowers on her mama and papa's grave and every body was telling her she could not go. I just went into the parlor to get away from all the fuss, and I was playing Jesus Loves Me when Mama and Daddy came down stairs. Mama was pleading with Daddy to please take Lil to the cemetery, and he kept saying "No," and he said it would be "Fool hardy" for anybody to go to the cemetery on a day like that. He also said that "Anybody with good sense would not even think about going." Well, Mama said Lil was beside herself, and one way or another she was going. I immediately went into Lil's bedroom and she was not beside herself, I cannot imagine how she could be. She was standing in front of her mirror, putting on her hat, and she already had on her fur coat and galoshes were on her high heels, and she was crying as hard as she could and for a change, she was very nice to me. She said "Darling, I have been to the cemetery every Christmas since Mama and Papa died, and I intend to do that as long as I live. You'll understand how I feel some day." Well, I certainly hoped I would not. I could not figure out how in the world my brain could possibly hold everything it was gonna have to understand, someday.

So, to make a long story short, Daddy said he would take Lil to the cemetery, because he had to go to the drug store and get cigarettes anyway. So he did, he put her out at the cemetery and told her that he would be back in fifteen minutes. She had her big funeral umbrella with her, but that had already turned inside out. She insisted that he go on and she told him that she would be ready to go home in fifteen minutes.

Well, the first person Daddy saw when he got to Cousin Elijah Perry's drugstore was Dr. Justus, he was a "crony" of Daddy's, and Mama did not care for him at all. Anyway, Doctor Justus invited Daddy to come upstairs to his office and have a glass of "cheer." So that's what he did, in fact, he had two or three glasses, and then he and his cigarettes went home.

Well, the minute he parted those rolling doors, everybody in the family wanted to know where Lil was. There was nothing he could do but admit that he had forgotten her. I'm telling you, you never heard such a commotion. Aunt Dolly just "swooned" in a dead faint right there in her big chair. Daddy said he was not going to waste any time apologizing; he was going back to get her immediately. And do you know what my Mama did? She made me go with him, just to make sure he came back. I tell you one thing; there was not much "cheer" in the house that day.

So Daddy and I got in the car, and he drove straight to the cemetery. By this time it had gotten dark, and the cemetery was not really any place I wanted to be at night, and it was snowing so hard you could hardly even see the tomb stones, but we got to our plot, and guess what? Lil was nowhere to be seen!!!! I thought to myself that Daddy was gonna keel over right there with a heart attack; his face got as white as that snow. We didn't know what to do, but we knew one thing we could not do and that was to go home without Lil. Colored town was close to the cemetery, and Matilda's mother lived in the first house, and I told Daddy to stop and ask her if she had seen Lil, and that's what we did. When we walked up on the porch I could see into her kitchen, and there sat Lil at the kitchen table drinking a cup of cocoa. That was a happy sight for sore eyes, let me tell you. Do you know that Lil was not even very mad with Daddy; she said she knew he would come sooner or later, so she just walked up to Matilda's house to wait.

When we got home everybody was so relieved they forgot to be mad with Daddy, and when we walked in the house there was a radio playing "Silent Night," and that was the most beautiful thing I had ever heard, and to this day, whenever I hear that song I think about that night so long ago.

Another thing that I will never forget was: This smell that you could not believe started coming from the butler's pantry. Now everybody knows this was that long room between the kitchen and the dining room. This room had a whole lot of shelves and a long counter, and that was where they kept the everyday china and silverware, and napkins and all kinds of preserves and relishes and stuff like that.

The ice box was in there, too. This was the kind of refrigerator that didn't make ice. (In fact, that kind hadn't even been invented yet.) Everyday the ice man would come and bring the ice. The ice would slowly melt and the water would go down underneath it into a pan that was under the ice box. Somebody, usually Wiggins Lee, had to empty that water everyday, or the pan would run over, which it did sometimes, and that was a mess.

Anyway, like I said, it was the most horrible smell in the world. Wiggins Lee came in and investigated, and he said it "Seemed like to him a rat had crawled inside the wall and died," and he thought that was where that smell was coming from.

Now, Lil was more afraid of rats than I was of spiders, and that was saying something. They had to give Lil smelling salts to revive her when she heard that, and she said that nobody could pay her to go in that pantry again "'til they got rid of that smell." She was very uneasy too; to think that there might be rats in the house.

My Daddy said that the only sensible thing to do was to tear out every cabinet in that room, and, if necessary, to go right into the wall and knock it down.

First of all, they had to take every thing out of those cabinets and throw it all away, because it was probably contaminated, and Lil said by all means, because she did not want anything, remotely, connected to that smell in the house, and everybody agreed with her. So Wiggins Lee and Matilda and Rosalie and Daddy and King King and I worked all day, and Wiggins Lee had this big fire going in the back yard, and every time he got a load he would take it straight out and put it on the fire. Well, let me tell you, there was a lot of stuff burned up that day.

When we finally got to the very last cabinet, and they were right on the verge of knocking that whole wall to smithereens, guess what? There, on the last shelf, was this little package of Limburger Cheese that Mama had gotten the last time she went to Henderson with Aunt Nora.

There was always something like this going on in our crazy family. Daddy said it was because they had inter-married so much.

King King and I went through torment almost, at meal time. They were always correcting us. Mama didn't care, she said we were children, and we would learn what we needed to know when we got older. But Aunt Dolly and Lil and Daddy were a different story all together. "Do not breathe while you're drinking out of a glass." "Close your mouth, and chew that food. I don't want to hear a word out of you, chew it 100 times." "Never, under any circumstances, take but one roll," "hold those elbows close to your side, you're not a bird, little girls can't fly", and just to me, "Hold your fork with your right hand, Willie Burton." I'm not kidding, it was hard.

Another thing that was totally unfair, I thought, was that we could not be excused from the table until every body finished. Now, that was bad anytime, because Lil ate just like a snail. She'd cut one little bitty piece of meat, slowly put it in her mouth, put her fork down and chew and chew and chew, and then she'd sort of sigh and pick her knife and fork up and do the same thing again.

I almost had a nervous breakdown, because I sat right next to her, and when Gertrude and Mary Ellen were out on the porch waiting for us to come out and play, it seemed like an eternity.

Finally, though, I just gave up, and started being slow like they were, and do you know, to this day, I am always the last one to finish eating everywhere I go. I'm right handed too, but it didn't come naturally, and I still do some things with my left hand.

Another thing they made us do was walk, for hours it seemed, with a book on our head. I would get so tired, for there were lots of other things I'd want to be doing. I did it so much though, that I believe I could have walked a thousand miles with a book on my head. Good posture was really stressed in our family, along with good grammar. Of course the most important thing was to tell the truth. Which I tried to do, you know, but sometimes it was almost impossible. For instance, I don't know if I would ever have told Daddy about going in the peach business with Cousin Tom's peaches if we hadn't broken out in a rash.

Well, now I'm gonna tell you something that really caused a lot of excitement. Like I have said before, nothing in our family was as important as family. For weeks I had been hearing about little Frank coming. I wondered who in the world was little Frank, and why on earth were they so excited about his coming.

Now, I don't think I have mentioned this before, but my great, great aunt Frankie (she was Grandpapa Billy's sister) was married to my great, great uncle, John Graham. Uncle John and Aunt Frankie had this, apparently, wonderful prep school for boys over in Warrenton, North Carolina, which was just 20 miles from Littleton. Some of the most successful and influential men in the state attended their school. It was a family institution. All of Aunt Frankie's and Uncle John's children taught there when they finished their own education. Most of my great aunts went to high school there before going to Littleton Female College, as did most of Aunt Frankie's other nieces and some select other young ladies, but it was primarily a boys' school. Some of my great aunts went back and taught over there before they got married. Aunt Dollie was the dietitian at the school when she was young, and all the boys just adored her.

This little Frank had gone to school at Uncle John's for several years and had spent a lot of weekends at my great grandparent's home. He was Uncle John's nephew besides, that's why they invited him in the first place, I guess. Well, he just fell in love with everybody in the family and came a lot, and they were very fond of him, too.

He was not a little boy at all, I found out. They called him "little Frank," because he was little. His whole name was Frank Porter Graham and he was the President of the University of North Carolina at Chapel Hill. He was coming to spend the weekend with Aunt Frankie, who was 96 at the time. All of her family came home for his visit, and some of them came from a long way off. Then on Saturday they were all coming over to Littleton and spend the day with us.

Aunt Ellen and all the rest of the great aunts that were still living decided to have this big family reunion in his honor. To tell you the truth, I still couldn't understand all the "to do." So many people were coming that it was decided that the grown ups would eat at Aunt Ellen's, and the little, insignificant children would have to stay at Aunt Dolly's and eat there. Rosalie and Matilda and Wiggins Lee were supposed to stay with us.

Anyway, the big day arrived and you never saw so many dressed up people in your life. They had all gone to Aunt Ellen's. Rosalie was out in our back yard with Wiggins Lee and Matilda. Each one of them had a big ice cream freezer, and they were just going to town turning those handles and laughing and having the best time you ever saw making the ice cream for the big event.

Well, what happened was this.

I went to the bathroom and when I flushed the commode, it kept on running. Well, I just simply panicked, 'cause I was so afraid it was gonna run over like it did one time and Daddy, thank goodness, was there, and he did something to make it stop and called the plumber, and the plumber came and fixed it. I was really at my wits end, so I went flying out in the back yard to get Rosalie, and she was having such a good time she wouldn't come. (In case, I haven't told you before, Rosalie was our nurse, and she was supposed to take care of us, but this time she did not.) She said they had to get that ice cream made, and just to let it run, that Daddy could fix it when he got home.

I could tell I was not gonna get any help from any of them, so I went back in the house. I didn't know what in the world to do, so I just simply went to the phone and told "central" that we had an emergency at Miss Dolly Daniel's on

Mosby Ave., and to please send some body fast. Well, she said, "Willie, where is Miss Dolly? Isn't she there?" and I said "no, they've all gone off and left me here by myself, and I am desperate." (I thought they would get somebody quicker, if they thought I was by myself.) Let me tell you that worked.

Up at Aunt Ellen's they were just getting ready to sit down to this sumptuous meal when all of a sudden these two fire trucks, (they just had two in Littleton) their sirens blaring, went flying by. Like I told you before, Aunt Ellen just lived two doors from Aunt Dolly.

Well, when they saw those fire trucks turn in at Aunt Dolly's, utter chaos broke out. I was standing on the front porch, getting ready to direct the firemen to the bath room, when I looked up and here came everybody!!!! Aunt Dolly's legs must have given out 'cause she was in front, and Daddy was on one side of her and Uncle William was on the other and they were trying to hold her up; she was almost in a dead faint. Lil was trying to run in those high heels, and Cousin Will Graham was trying to steer her in the right direction.

Well, you never saw so many people, women and men, who looked like they were on the verge of fainting! I do not, honestly, believe the people on the Titanic, when it was getting ready to sink, could have been much more distraught.

You see, this is how it was. That house had already burned to the ground two times, and they lived in mortal terror that it might happen again. I told you about all those antiques and family portraits that they had had a terrible time saving before.

I guess they could have killed me, right then and there, 'cause when they got back to Aunt Ellen's all the food had gotten cold, and the ice cream had melted. I, personally, think it kinda served them right, 'cause if they had treated us like human beings and invited us to eat with the rest of the family, we would not have even been at Aunt Dolly's by our selves. It still took them a long time to forgive me.

I told you I had decided to get into show business, remember? Now everybody said what a sweet voice I had. I got that from Mama; she had studied voice for years, and was going to Boston Conservatory, 'til she met my Daddy, and fell in love and got married.

Well, I didn't know if just a sweet voice was gonna get me in show business, and so I decided to be a "torch" singer, like Libby Holman on the radio. I would go in the bathroom and put my feet on the little foot stool that Mama had in there for King King and me. I would practice and practice singing as low as I could, and do you know it worked! I didn't grow to be very big for a long time, but I'll tell you I had a big, low voice. I had been singing in Sunday school for years, and Miss Lottie Latham, the organist at church could not understand what was happening to my voice. Anyway, right there in Aunt Dolly's bathroom, I turned into a "torch" singer. I'll explain more about that later.

Uncle Rich ♫

You will never guess in a million years who was sitting in the back living room when I got home from school yesterday. It was my uncle Rich!!!! Richards Kingsland Daniel, the only brother of my grandmamma Willie and all my great aunts. I told you he was a wild man; well, he didn't look wild, he just looked handsome! He bore a striking resemblance to that movie star, John Barrymore, only he was better looking, 'cause he was very tall and just like the rest of my family, he held his head up high and stood as straight as an arrow. Of course he was pretty old, in his forty's I think

Well, he certainly did not look like a convict, and that's what I had decided he must be, because I overheard Lil say one day: (when she didn't know I was in hearing distance, she was talking to Mama, and she said) "No, Fannie Kingsland, I will never be able to forgive Rich, for you know he killed Mama." Well, I couldn't ask them anything about it, because I didn't want them to know that I had overheard what she said and nobody ever told me he was on the chain gang, but isn't that where they send people who kill people? I certainly could not blame Lil for not forgiving him 'cause I would never forgive anybody if they killed my mama.

Anyway, here he was in Littleton, and I couldn't even ask him about being a convict, but he told me about a lot of things, about all the places in the world he had been. To tell you the truth, I could not help liking him even if he had killed my great grandmamma.

He didn't stay very long; Aunt Dollie said he never did. He would just blow in one day, and a few days later he'd blow out again, and nobody would hear from him again for a very long time. They loved him though, I could tell; sometimes when Aunt Dollie talked about him tears would come in her eyes.

After he left I got my nerve up, and I confessed to Mama about what I had heard Lil say, and Mama was not even mad. She put her arms around me, and she said, "No, Billie Bett", (that's what she called me when she was not mad with me.) She said, "Uncle Rich didn't literally kill Grandma, but he worried her to death, and they had had such high hopes for him, and she had to sell thousands of acres of her Kingsland land to get him out of trouble, and he broke her heart"

Well, I saw my Uncle Rich several times after that, he would show up, and then he'd be gone again, and when I was almost a grown woman Aunt Dollie received a letter from a Veteran's hospital in California, (he had been in the Spanish American war) saying that he had died. And you know I have found out that, generally, the ones who cause us the most heartache are the ones we love the most. At least, that's how it's been for me.

Daddy Gets Sick 🎵

But now to get on with my story; you might say our trouble began when Daddy got sick. Does it seem strange to you how things can start to change, and you don't even know they're changing, and then all of a sudden nothing is like it used to be. Well, this is how it happened.

Daddy, for a long time had had kidney trouble, but then all of a sudden it got real bad. Dr. Justus would come two or three times a day 'cause he was real sick. I'd go in his room when I could and sit with him, and I would sing to him, "When Your Hair Has Turned to Silver" and "The Valley of the Moon." They were the ones he liked for me to sing the most. King King would recite her poem, "Me Like a Bow Wow", (it was the only poem she knew, but it was Daddy's favorite poem.) Dr. Justus finally told Daddy he was sorry but he had to quit driving. Now, he could ride in a car, but he could not drive a car. So, that's when Daddy got Weldon White.

It was funny for Weldon's last name to be White, 'cause he was as black as the ace of spades. We were just crazy about him. I am telling you, he really could play the piano too. Daddy told everybody that Weldon could tear a piano to pieces, but he did not tear it to pieces. Lil really would have been mad if he did!

Daddy and Weldon started going out to call on customers, but more and more, Daddy would be drinking when he came home, and it just about drove Mama crazy. She cried and she fussed, I told you what a good fusser she was. Everybody was getting mad with Daddy. Business was really beginning to fall off, and they all blamed Daddy. Of course, the depression was in full force, and that probably had a lot to do with business.

That depression was something, I'll tell you. It was late coming to Littleton, but it came. Everyday at least one, sometimes two or three poor old tramps would be sitting on the back steps eating whatever Aunt Dollie and Matilda would fix for them. Daddy said you couldn't drive down the highway without seeing women and children along the side of the road just trying to get anywhere they knew somebody who might give them a place to stay and something to eat.

When we would go to ride on Sunday, we would always stop and pick up somebody and take them, at least, as far as we were going, and Daddy would reach in his pocket and give them a dollar or two. There was no welfare then. Churches would try to help people, but they ran out of money. Times were hard; I don't think people today have any idea just how hard.

Well, it was baseball season, and if there was anything my Daddy really liked, it was baseball. So, when Daddy should have been tending to business, he and Weldon would go by and pick up Dr. Justus and off they'd go, if a ball game was anywhere within a hundred miles, and when they got home you could tell he'd been drinking. The way I could tell was that when he drank, he acted silly, not like my Daddy at all. Daddy was very dignified, the way a Daddy should be, but when he drank it changed him completely.

It kept getting worse and worse, and everybody in the family was mad with Daddy, except King King and me. Business just kept falling off, and a lot of people owed them money. The person in charge of the radio program they were sponsoring absconded with a whole lot of money. Finally, the business was forced to declare bankruptcy. Mama was mortified. Aunt Dollie was furious with Daddy and told him he had to leave, and that just broke my heart, and Daddy's, too. He had been paying a whole lot of money for us to live there, and he couldn't anymore. Aunt Dollie and Lil did not want Mama and King King and me to leave, but Uncle William insisted that he pay board for us if we stayed there. The truth was Aunt

Dollie and Lil didn't have very much money. When the banks closed they lost everything. Just try to imagine how it would be, if you had enough money in the bank to live comfortably for the rest of your life, and then one day the bank just closed, and there was no way to ever get your money out. It was almost as bad as the Civil War, that is when my family really suffered, for my family had lots of land, and there was nobody to work it anymore. Times were hard, I'll tell you.

Mama's heart was broken, besides, she was embarrassed to death. She told Uncle William she just couldn't stay in Littleton anymore. Some good friends of hers had moved to Charlotte, and they wanted her to stay with them 'til she got on her feet. Uncle William told her to go on to Charlotte, if that was what she thought she should do, and he told her he would send King King and me to a boarding school in Virginia. Mama wouldn't hear of that, though. She left us with Aunt Dollie and Lil and said she would send for us just as soon as she possibly could. Uncle William paid for us to stay with Aunt Dollie and Lil. They'd have kept us anyway, I know, but money was scarce.

Daddy was in a place for alcoholics, Uncle William had seen to that. We didn't know if we would ever see him again.

Mama got a job right away, and she had never worked a day in her life, but my Mama was mighty pretty. And so she just walked into this upscale dress shop and asked for a job, and they hired her right away. Every letter we got would have a dollar in it, and it would make me cry. Right then, when I was nine years old, I changed from being Mama's little girl to being her protector. I was determined that somehow I was gonna help her.

I really missed her, let me tell you. I'd wake up in the middle of the night and hear the train whistle and hope so hard that she was coming home. She did come one time, but I cried the whole time she was there, cause I didn't want her to go back,

We were very well cared for, we loved Aunt Dollie and Lil and all the rest of our aunts and uncles, but it was not like when Mama and Daddy were there. I wrote to Mama two or three times a week and told her how much we missed her, but Aunt Dollie said not to worry her, that she knew we missed her, and she missed us too, and she would send for us just as soon as she could.

Anyway, finally!!!! A letter came saying she was ready for us to come, well, happy days were here again. I couldn't wait to go. I just knew we would have a beautiful home, and I knew that a great big city like Charlotte would have a place for me to get started in show business.

I will never forget the day King King and I went to Charlotte. We got up early and had a big breakfast, which I was too excited to eat. Aunt Dollie fixed us a lunch to eat on the train, fried chicken and pimento sandwiches. Lil was crying, and tears were in Aunt Dollie's eyes. They hated to see us go I know, 'cause we were almost like their own. King King was crying, too. She loved Littleton, so did I, but I loved Mama more, and I thought she needed me.

Buck Harris, Uncle William's man, came right on the dot, (he said he'd be there at 8:30, and he was) and took us to Raleigh. When we got to the train depot he bought our tickets to Charlotte and got on the train with us and talked to the Conductor, and the Conductor came and talked to us and told us we were in his care. "So, young ladies, just sit back and enjoy your trip, and you'll be in Charlotte before you know it." Well, it took us forever to get there! I must have asked the Conductor 100 times, "Are we nearly there?" and he'd pat me on the head and say, "No, but it won't be long now." After what seemed like forever he came and said, "all right, children, let's get everything together, we're pulling into the station." He was a very nice man; I'll always hold Conductors in high regard. We had a drumstick left over from our lunch, and I presented it to him. King King said that was what we should do, 'cause she said I had worried the poor man to death.

Anyway, we were in Charlotte!!!! I looked out the window, and I could not believe it, there stood my Daddy!!!!!! Happy days were here again!!!!!

Daddy had a taxi waiting and took us home. I was so excited! I could hardly wait to see Mama and our beautiful new home. Well, the taxi pulled up in front of a house that was not so beautiful. In truth, it had been beautiful in its day, in fact, it was an old mansion that had been turned into an apartment house, and the neighborhood that surrounded it was beginning to not be so good. Daddy explained the neighbors were very nice people but that they were working people and that we'd grow to like them. He opened the front door to a huge hall, and a beautiful stairway, and he said, "All right children, let's go upstairs and see Mama. He opened a door, and there was Mama standing up at an ironing board and ironing!!!! I didn't know Mama even knew how to iron! Well, anyway, we were so glad to see her! It didn't matter about the house, nothing mattered except we were all together again, and before you knew it we had adjusted to our new life, but let me tell you, it was different.

And so we moved to Charlotte, smack dab, in the middle of the Depression. I was nine, my sister, Kingsland, had just turned eight.

Up until then money was not an item. It's not until you don't have it that you miss it, and I guess, maybe, you miss it more if you've always had plenty. Not that we had ever possessed great wealth, there had just always been enough and for many generations. Before the Civil War my family had been quite well to do.

The worst thing was that Mama had to work, and I thought that was terrible. My mama was just not supposed to work. Well, she was too pretty to have to work, and she would come home so tired. She'd always have to lie down for a while when she got home, before she had to get up and fix supper.

Daddy worked too, of course, but then men were supposed to do that, but he would be mighty tired when he got home, 'cause now he didn't have a driver to take him around and do errands for him. Well, my goodness, he didn't even have a car to drive himself; he had to ride the streetcar or walk. But I'll say this for him, Daddy tried to help Mama. In fact, he'd always get up early and fix breakfast for us. My daddy loved my mama very much.

I've told you what a good fusser my mama was, well, she kept getting better and better at it, until I would say she was an expert.

She thought she was too pretty to have to work too, and she told my daddy that no woman in her family had ever had to lift a finger and do any work. My mama told my daddy a thousand times that she had married beneath her, and she could only imagine how disappointed her papa must be. That she knew he was turning over in his grave.

But still I know Mama loved Daddy. She just had to fuss sometimes, besides that, she had been so embarrassed and humiliated when he drank and the business failed.

Anyway, here we were in Charlotte, in the middle of the depression, and I couldn't do anything about it, because I was still a little girl, and it seemed to me I had been a little girl long enough. I made up my mind that if I ever did grow up, I was gonna do something to help my mama. I wasn't too pretty to work, in fact, I wasn't even pretty at all, but I was gonna be when I grew up. I heard Elizabeth Burton tell Mama one day,

"Why, Fanny Kingsland, Bill (she was to first one to call me Bill) is going to be very nice looking when she grows up. Blondes are very sought after these days."

Well, Mama really did not want to have a blond child, and she always had Rosalie to rinse my hair in tea when she washed it. For the life of me I don't know why she married a blonde man if she didn't want a blonde child. To tell you the truth, I was kinda glad it was blonde, because in movie books Jean Harlot was my favorite movie star, and her hair was as white as cotton. So I made up my mind that when I grew up I'd get a permanent wave and have curly light blond hair and wear bright red lipstick like Jean Harlot and be a movie star and a torch singer like Libby Holman. But the first thing I'd do would be to buy a beautiful home for my mama and daddy, and have a house full of servants again.

Charlotte could not possibly have been more different from Littleton. In Littleton everybody knew who we were, and nobody in Charlotte knew us. In Littleton the most important thing besides telling the truth was good grammar and to stand up straight and hold your shoulders back. In Charlotte the children, most of them anyway, used terrible grammar, you wouldn't believe the way they talked: "I seen," "I taken," "I come," and "I ain't." I'm telling you it was unbelievable. My mama and daddy would kill me if I talked like that. And on top of that, they made fun of the way I talked, because of my Virginia brogue. Believe me, it would be a cold day in, you know where, before I would ever talk like them.

There is no good way a child can make money, so I just decided we'd have to be poor for a while. In the meantime, though, I practiced singing as low as I could, so that when the time came I'd be ready. Every Saturday I sang in the Popeye Club Amateur Contest, and Kingsland would recite her poem, Me Like a Bow Wow. That way we got in the movies free, and that saved a whole dime. Sometimes I'd win the prize, a whole dollar bill. When I did Kingsland and I would go shopping at the 10 cents store, and buy Mama presents. We bought her I don't know how many bottles of Blue Waltz Perfume. (I never did smell it on her though; she said she was saving it for a special occasion.)

I also would go downtown and pay the light bill and the water bill for some of the neighbors, Mrs. Dwelle next door, and Mrs. Cook, who lived in the other upstairs apartment, and Sue Patterson who lived down stairs with her husband, Bob and their little boy, Bobby, who was my age, and they would pay me a whole nickel every time.. When we got older, Daddy would buy a whole crate of Pepsi Colas and Orange Crush and Ne-Hi Grape, and we'd put ice in our red wagon and put the drinks in the ice and pull the wagon to the tennis court and you'd be amazed how many drinks we sold. In fact, we made so much money I told Mama and Daddy we didn't need the twenty five cents they gave each of us every week for our allowance.

Daddy and Mama wouldn't hear of that though, but Daddy said we ought to save our allowance for a rainy day. That didn't make a lot of sense to me, because on rainy days you couldn't go anywhere to even spend money.

In the summer time we'd go back to Littleton and sometimes stay the whole summer with Aunt Dollie and Lil. Daddy would put us on the train in the conductor's care, and Buck would meet us in Norlina. Aunt Dollie and Lil were always with him. We looked forward all year to going; it really was almost like heaven. Everybody seemed so glad to see us, and we were so glad to see them. I really loved my kin people. It's funny, but you don't feel as close to anybody as you do your own people.

We couldn't breathe it to a soul though, that Daddy was in Charlotte. That made it a little bit uncomfortable. My Uncle William was really mad with my daddy.

Much as we loved Littleton, it was always good to go back to Charlotte and be with Mama and Daddy.

Daddy got a better job, traveling for a drug company. Mama got an easier job; she'd go around to all the sewing rooms (that Roosevelt had started to ease the strain of the depression on poor people) and play the piano and sing and lead them in singing. I went with her a lot when I wasn't in school, and I would sing for the ladies. Then Mama would have a party for them. It was a lot of fun. I loved to ride the streetcar, and I thought that singing for the ladies would help me in my singing career, whenever I got a singing career.

On the days when I would go with Mama, Kingsland and her cat would go with Daddy. She and Herbert Hoover II would sit in the car while Daddy went in and called on his customers and listen to the radio. One day she came home so excited she didn't know what to do. She said they'd announced on the Briar Hopper program that they were looking for a little girl and boy to sing on the show. Well, this was my golden opportunity. I cried and carried on something awful, before I got Daddy to write an excuse so I could get out of school early and go try out. (I overheard Mama tell Daddy it wouldn't hurt to let me go, because they probably wouldn't choose me, anyway.

Well, she was mistaken, there were about a million children trying out, and everybody but me had at least one parent with them. To tell you the truth, I was scared to death, some of those children were all dressed up in cowboy boots and had on make up and looked just beautiful. I just looked like a little girl, and my mama wouldn't dream of letting me wear makeup. Anyway, they called my number and I went in this big studio, and I nearly fainted when I saw the piano player. He was the same one who used to play for the Popeye Club. Well, for some reason, he'd always liked me. He told me to sing Bill Bailey, and that's what I did. There was nobody else in that big studio but Clarence, the piano player and me, but this voice came out of nowhere and asked me what my name was, and I said, just as plain as I could, Billie Burton, (I wasn't about to tell them it was Willie) then the voice asked me if I knew 20 songs. Now I don't like to tell stories, but sometimes you just have to, and besides, I knew I could learn 20 songs, so I crossed my fingers and said, "Yes, sir, I do." Then the voice told me to go out and sit down in the lobby and wait, which is what I did. This man I knew, he lived next door to us at Mrs. Peterson's boarding house, I didn't even know he worked at WBT, came out and told me not to go anywhere, Well, I wasn't about to go anywhere. So, I just sat there and kept saying my prayers that they would like me enough to let me win. After a while there was nobody waiting except this boy about 14 and his daddy and me.

Finally, another man came out and told this boy and me to come with him back in the studio. Well, this time there were lots of men in there. They told us to come back the next day and sing on the program.

Sweetheart of the Carolinas

I'm telling you, I could hardly wait to get home to tell Mama and Daddy. Well, they were almost as excited as I was, and I had been afraid that they might say I couldn't do it. That night Daddy taught me a song, Let the Rest of the World Go By. That's what I sang the next day on the program, and they seemed to like it. They told us to come back the next day, and the next day they told us to come back the next day.

We had been on the program for a week. When I got off the elevator that day, the boy, Homer, was waiting. He told me to go back to the payroll department and get my check. I didn't know where the payroll department was, but I asked and when I got there they gave me a check for ten dollars. I was flabbergasted! This was too good to be true, that was more than my mama even made.

I really couldn't wait to get home that day; I even paid seven cents and rode the bus. Mama was in the kitchen getting ready to start supper, and I rushed in and told her that now we could have a cook again, and I gave her the check.

A Wonderful Part of My Life ♫

I couldn't believe that this was really happening. I was just so happy. I loved singing. You just cannot know how much I enjoyed it. This was as good as it could get, and I knew it. They called me the 'Sweetheart of the Carolinas' and the 'Carolina Sunshine Girl,' and what I liked best of all, 'The Youngest and the Last of the Blues Singers.'

The "Briar Hoppers" was the most popular show in North Carolina, and we got mail from Maine, and even from Cuba. WBT was a powerful station, made even more powerful because its tower was on top of Mount Mitchell. In those days there were not all that many radio stations, in fact there were very few, especially big ones. They didn't play records on the radio, then. Every station had its own staff of musicians, and every show was live. WBT afforded the very best musicians, and the best announcers. Every studio was equipped with a Steinway Grand.

I remember 'Dad' (Johnny McAllister) saying that if radio stations were ever allowed to play records on the air it would mean the end of local shows. He was right

The "Briar Hoppers" show was a variety show. There was not a single, real "hillbilly" on it. They played all kinds of music, some country, certainly, but mostly, the music of that day and time; the really "good" songs that are the standards of today.

Bill Davis played the 'fiddle' on the show and could really play some 'ho downs,' in reality he was a concert violinist and played with the North Carolina Symphony. All the musicians were equally good, all were accomplished musicians. I was so lucky to have been 'brought up' by them and to have worked so closely with them. They were exceptionally nice to me; they never forgot that I was a child. Not one of them ever said a bad word or told a bad joke in front of me. Children then were protected from stark reality. Innocence prevailed.

I absolutely loved being on that program. It came on every day at four o'clock and lasted for an hour. It was on six days a week, Monday through Saturday. I never tired of it, and it consumed most of my time, for by the second year we had begun going on 'personal appearances.'

The format of the show was a family. The patriarch was "Dad", (Johnny McAllister) and his family, five grown sons, a grown daughter, and the children on the show, his little girl, Billie, (me) and teen aged boy, Homer. I was crazy about all of

68

my "big brothers" and my big sister, Minnie, (Jane Bartlett) but was always just a little in awe, of "Dad." Charlie Crutchfield was the announcer, and he was the funniest thing in the world. He made fun of the sponsor all the time, and they loved him. The rapport between "Dad" and "Charlie" was hilarious!

Everything on that show just seemed to "click." Homer soon became a teen age "idol." The girls went "wild" for him, and the mail just poured in. We were sponsored by Drug Trade Products, and they seemed very pleased with the show. I got lots of mail, too. I didn't see much of it, it was sent to the sponsor, but Grady Cole told Daddy I got 2500 letters one day. We also received presents, boxes of home made cookies, candy and even flowers.

The second year my salary went up to fifteen dollars a week, plus whatever I made on personal appearances. We always played to a packed house, but you've got to remember, tickets ranged from twenty five cents to seventy five cents, so nobody got rich. I averaged, though, about thirty five dollars a week, and that was very good for those days.

I have so many, many happy memories of that part of my life. I didn't always like the songs I had to sing, but I had to sing the most requested songs. Dad, though, was good; he'd nearly always let me do one song I really liked. Personal

Appearances were lots of fun too. I suppose I've been in every town, in every school, (The only auditorium in some towns was the school house) in every auditorium plus a lot of courthouses (The biggest auditorium is some places was the court room) in the Piedmont and the western part of North and South Carolina and Virginia. We got to one place one night, way back in the mountains, and they didn't even have electricity. I couldn't sing, because the P A wouldn't work. Sometimes we'd get to a place and they'd have a spread you wouldn't believe. Country ham and fried chicken and homemade pies and cakes and everything were so good. Usually though, if we weren't going too far, Clarence would take me to Thacker's Restaurant to eat before we left and Clarence would order for me. Sometimes Dad would go with us. He'd always order a steak for me; he thought I was too thin. Sometimes we'd stop along the way and eat, and on the way home at night too.

Homer and I waited in the wings while the show was going on until Dad would call us out to do our songs. We never got tired of watching, and we'd laugh at the same jokes we'd heard so many times before. Sometimes we'd play games. We loved Hide and Seek. One time I was hiding up in a sort of loft, you had to climb up a ladder to get up there, and Homer moved the ladder and when Dad called me out to sing I couldn't get down. One time we were playing 'Tag,' running behind the stage, and we knocked the scenery down on top of everybody. Dad didn't think that was very funny. Oh, I can think of a million things. One thing I'll always remember. We had a show, way up in the mountains, in Boone. Boone was just a small town then. It was the worst weather imaginable, snowing hard with ice everywhere. It took us a long time to get there. We didn't even have time to stop and eat. The show was in the Courthouse, and Homer and I waited in the Judge's office. There was a big burlap bag filled with apples, and Homer and I were hungry. We had a race to see who could eat the most apples. I got the worst stomach ache, and when Dad called me out to sing I was almost doubled over with pain. After the show the Highway Petrol came and told us we would not be able to get back to Charlotte that night, that the roads were just a solid sheet of ice. Well, I told them we had to go, because my Daddy hadn't even wanted me to go that day because the weather was so bad. So finally they decided to try to make it, but you know what I did? I was sort of scared too, so I made all those men get down on their knees and pray that we'd get home safely. There was a big old pot bellied stove, and we all knelt down around it. Bill Davis fell over laughing, and soon they were all laughing except me. We made it home, though. When I told Daddy he said we should have listened to the Highway Patrol, that it was a wonder we had made it.

Everyday I could hardly wait to go to the broadcasting station. I just loved it, and I was awfully glad to be making money too.

I never thought about it being my money. Every pay day though, I'd splurge and get a banana split for fifteen cents, and it was soooo good! Back in those days, there were no substitutes. Real whipped cream and lots of it. Then, if we were not going on a personal appearance, I'd walk home and go by the butcher shop and buy four t-bone steaks (they were thirty nine cents a pound then) and then I'd go across the street to the bakery and buy French rolls and take them home to Mama with the rest of the money. I seldom rode the bus home and we lived in the Elizabeth section, which was quite far out. I spent my bus fare on peanuts so I could stop at the pet store and feed the monkeys.

Clarence Etters was the pianist on the show, and I worked more closely with him than with any of the others. Many times when I got to the studio and looked at the program I would find that I was scheduled to sing at least one, sometimes two songs that I'd never heard before. I didn't get out of school until three o'clock. By the time I caught the bus down town it was always at least three twenty when I got to the broadcasting station, and the program came on at four. So in those forty minutes I had to learn sometimes two songs. I never did learn to read music, but Clarence would play the melody and we'd go over it two or three times and by four o'clock I usually knew the songs well enough to sing them that day.

Clarence quickly became my mentor. I thought he was just wonderful, and he was, to me. He was the best friend I've ever had. Clarence had a tremendous influence on my life. I tried my level best to please him, and for many years I did. He had high hopes for me and thought I was really going to "go" places. I disappointed him, terribly. I disappointed lots of people, but I'll get to that later, too.

Those Briar Hopper days were wonderful. Of course, I missed a lot. Fact is I never was a teenager. I never had a "boy friend", never really even "saw" boys. Clarence hated "boy crazy girls," so even if I'd been inclined to like them, I wouldn't have, and it embarrassed me to death if boys acted like they liked me, because I didn't want Clarence to think I had done anything to attract them.

When I was on stage, it was o. k. to flirt, in fact Clarence showed me how. I'd pick out some little boy in the front row and "make eyes" at him, and everybody would laugh, and the little boy would turn red, and I'll bet it embarrassed him, but when I wasn't on stage, I just pretended not to see boys, and that's the way Clarence liked it, and "Dad," Johnny McAllister, too. I look back and see that little girl that was me so long ago, and it almost seems like a dream. I was not a very precocious child. The only person I really got to know was Clarence. When somebody asked me a question, I answered, but I never expressed an opinion of my own. I knew my place, I was a child, and I acted like a child.

I didn't wear make-up, not even lipstick 'til I was 16, not even on the stage. No matter how late it was when I got home from personal appearances, Mama would get up and roll my hair, and no matter how late it was I had to get up early and go to school. If I really was sick and didn't go to school I'd usually feel better by the time I was supposed to go to the broadcasting station, and on those days I would always dedicate my songs to Dr. Elliott, the Principal. I knew he'd be listening. I loved Dr. Elliott. He was my friend.

I loved the grown-ups on the show, all the musicians and Mr. Crutchfield, and later the other announcers, but I was always a little in awe of them, and I never, really, got on familiar terms with them.

One day, when I was 16, Mr. Crutchfield, who now was the station manager, called me into his office and told me they were taking me off the show because I wasn't a little girl

74

anymore and they needed somebody who could, and would, sing country, that country music was the coming thing. He knew I didn't like country music. I just didn't understand it, and I couldn't, I wouldn't sing it. Well, that just broke my heart, besides that, it made me mad, and I really did not want to leave the show.

I still can't believe I did this, but I did, and I persuaded Clarence to go along with it, too. I disguised my voice and called and made an appointment to have an audition for the program. I told them my name was Sally Ruth Perkins. Clarence and I went into one of the smaller studios on the appointed day. Mr. Crutchfield was in his office (like I knew he would be) listening, so he couldn't see me. I sang 'Beautiful Brown Eyes" like it had never been sung before. I mean I just really twanged it up. It was TERRIBLE! Nothing ever was uglier than that. Do you know what Mr. Crutchfield did? He LOVED it. He said I was exactly what he'd been looking for, and he hired me right on the spot. Well, I was glad and I was sad. I was glad to still be on the program, but I was sad, because I absolutely did not want to sing like that.

It took a lot of nerve to go up to the station that first day, I was kinda worried, too, that Mr. Crutchfield might be mad when he found out it was me. Anyway, I took the bull by the horns and went up there and went into the studio. Well, everybody seemed glad to see me, (I still hadn't seen Mr. Crutchfield) and I was just getting up my nerve to look at the program to see what I was scheduled to sing when out of nowhere I heard Mr. Crutchield's voice. He said, "Miss Perkins, we're so glad to have you on the show, but I want you to sing as much like Billie as you can." He had known all along, and instead of Clarence and me pulling one over on him, he and Clarence had really pulled one over on me.

I wonder sometimes, what my life would have been like, if I'd never been on the program. Certainly, more normal, I suppose, but I was on the program, so who knows.

I was on that show until I was seventeen, and when I was seventeen I was almost exactly like I had been when I was twelve. I knew no more about life or the real world. It was almost like I had been in a cocoon. I didn't want to ever grow up, because I just loved my life the way it was. I didn't have to grow up now to help Mama. I was already helping her. Of course, I would liked to have made more money so I could help her more and she could stop work, but that would come in time, I supposed. Meantime, I just enjoyed being a child, and a singing child at that. Homer told me, years later, that he really liked me a lot, but they told him if he ever told me that he did, they'd take him off the show. To tell you the truth, I would not have liked him if he had told me, but I was very fond of him, I loved them all.

I grew a whole foot when I was fifteen. When I started on the show I was 4'7', which explains, I suppose, why they called me "little" Billie. When I left the show, I was 5'7", which was quite tall for a girl in those days. By the time I was seventeen, country music was really coming into its own. Johnny McAllister had left the show a year earlier, and Clarence wasn't on it, anymore. He was Music Director for the station. And we had our own show on Sundays, but the whole Briar Hopper program had changed. Fact is, there were some real country musicians on the program now, and I just couldn't sing country. So when Daddy wanted to move to Wilmington I was ready to go.

One of my favorite songs I did on the program was "Look Down That Lonesome Road." Oh, how I wish I could go back "up" that road, but we don't ever get that chance, we just have to keep going, even when it seems sort of pointless. We take what comes, and we go on. And we try not to let the pain that we endure leave a scar.

The United States was preparing to go to war long before December 7, 1941. Every morning, when I would be getting ready for school, there was nothing on the news but the war in Europe. We had been hearing about Hitler's soldiers demolishing the streets and countryside of Europe, about the bombs falling on London, the destruction and the loss of life they wreaked. We knew it was only a matter of time, in fact, we wondered why we were not already involved. Army camps and defense programs were springing up all over the country. Civilians were busy building bomb shelters in their basements. People, for months, had been hoarding canned goods and staples with which to stock these shelters.

Wilmington was chosen as the site of The North Carolina Shipbuilding Co. It opened its doors in 1941, and was seeking employees to build sea going (Liberty) ships which would be needed if we did, in fact, go to war. Overnight, this beautiful little city became a boom town. Jobs were plentiful, pay was good and it became a Mecca for many from all walks of life. Not only did the shipyard draw people, Camp Davis, a large army camp, sprang to life at Holly Ridge, a suburb of

Wilmington. Blumenthal Air Force Base, a training ground for fighter pilots, was just outside of Wilmington.

We moved to Wilmington, which was ill prepared for the influx of people, in the early, early summer of 1941. Housing was at a premium. People, who lived here, lived in their own homes. There was no need for apartments and very little need for rental property. When the need arose, however, construction began quickly, and suitable housing became plentiful. Daddy, who had never done any construction work in his life, secured a position as supervisor in the Erector's department at the shipyard.

We found Wilmington to be a wonderful place to live. We had lots of relatives there. Aunt Minnie and Uncle Carr and Ann and Mary Daniel had come here directly from Littleton, even before we went to Charlotte. They had a beautiful, big (eighteen rooms) home which they had bought soon after moving here. We stayed with them for a while until we found a place of our own. We loved being able to go to the beach every day, and it was so good just to bump into relatives again. I had missed that in Charlotte.

There was something about Wilmington that was very exciting in those days. We were on the brink of war. We didn't know when, but we knew it was coming. You could almost feel it. Maybe we intuitively sensed that life must be lived to the fullest, because the way of life we had known was soon to be ended.

There were wonderful seafood places to eat, located way out on the sound, places that specialized in oyster roast, all you could eat, with little boys who did nothing but stand beside every plate and open the oysters and drop them into bowls of melted butter. Miss Janie's, my favorite, also served the most delicious clam fritters and hush puppies. Every seafood place was good, though, everything was fresh. In those days there was no such thing as frozen seafood.

I was over at Aunt Minnie's that Sunday afternoon, waiting for Mary Daniel to get ready so we could go for a ride, when the announcement came on the radio. The Japanese had bombed Pearl Harbor!!!! Well, the whole world just exploded! The excitement was indescribable! Uncle Carr was down in the basement working on his bomb shelter. I flew downstairs and then down to the basement to tell him. He couldn't believe it, nobody could. It was unbelievable! We knew it was coming, but I don't think anybody really thought it was coming, and here it was; there was no question, this meant war! Overnight, the whole world changed.

I had made up my mind to be a Red Cross Nurse. You know, like the song says, "Mid the wars great curse, stands the Red Cross Nurse. She's the rose of no man's land." (I used to sing it.) I thought that would be a good thing to be. But then I heard you had to cut your hair to do that, so I decided I wouldn't. Anyway, I'll tell you the truth, I was so busy I would not have had time.

My mama, who had never canned a thing in her whole life, had me standing in line, for hours, to get canning sugar; (That was the only way you could get enough sugar,) then she had to learn to can, so I wouldn't be telling a story. The only thing she ever canned, though, was some pears that grew out in our yard. Well, then you had sign up for ration books for every thing practically, butter and beef and even shoes. It was unbelievable! You couldn't buy Coca Colas, (those victory colas were so bad, though, that that didn't matter), but even candy. Imagine not being able to even buy a Hershey Bar, and Hershey Bars were so good then, made with real chocolate. It was just unbelievable!

I got tired of that war pretty fast, and another thing I thought of, suppose the man I was supposed to marry got killed in the war before I even met him. I knew exactly how he was going to look, and I was really looking forward to meeting him.

Sweetheart of the Carolinas

All of a sudden, there was a big USO downtown, and all the girls were going to dance with the soldiers and be patriotic. Aunt Minnie let Mary Daniel and Ann go, but Daddy wouldn't let me go, he said I could find other ways to be patriotic. Sometimes, though, when I'd spend the night at Aunt Minnie's, I would go, but I didn't see anybody who looked like my Prince Charming. Ann told me if I ever did see him to look at the back of his head and say over and over, to myself, "You like me, you're just crazy about me," that that was the way to hypnotize them. I never did forget that. Sometimes, I'd just practice on somebody to see if it really worked, and you know, it really did. So, all I had to do was see him, and then I'd live happily ever after. Wouldn't it be wonderful if life really was like that?

This big, new supper club, opened up in early 1942. I had never even been in a night club before, but I decided I was getting old enough to sing in one. Well, the papers were full of what a wonderful place it was, and there were pictures of the people who worked out there. The singer was Grace Lee. I saw her once downtown in the drug store, and she was beautiful. Her hair was almost as white as cotton, and she looked a lot like Lana Turner. Her husband had the orchestra out there, so I just decided to give up on that idea. Well, then I heard that this Grace Lee and her husband were no longer there. Something happened, I don't know what. This looked, to me, like a golden opportunity.

Ann's boy friend, (who later became her husband) Bobby Gaylord, knew the new manager at this, the Plantation Club, so I asked him to please take me out there so I could audition. Well, he did. Ann and Bobby and I went out there and I met Jimmy Jett, the manager.

He was sitting at a table eating his supper when we got there. He invited us to sit down and ordered a coca cola for each of us. He didn't say very much. He was listening to the new orchestra and asked me how I liked it. It was wonderful! And I told him so. I was really nervous, and I just sat there tearing up my cocktail napkin in little bitty pieces (like Gertrude and I did that time,) only this time I didn't even realize I was doing it. Well, Jimmy acted like he didn't notice that I'd been doing it either, but when I had it all torn up, he called the head waiter over and asked him to bring another napkin, then he didn't even turn around, he just shoved it over to me and said now I could start on that one.

I was really nervous, you know there are a lot of gangsters around night clubs, but I was trying to act sophisticated, and like I wasn't scared at all. Jimmy told me he was from Charlotte too, and that he remembered me when I was a little girl, and really enjoyed my singing. Then he got up and went over and got on the band stand and he sang, "This Is the Story of a Starry Night," and it was the most beautiful thing I had ever heard, and he had the most beautiful voice I have ever heard, to this day, and then he announced that I was going to sing, and by this time, I wasn't nervous at all, and I got up and sang, and got the job.

Imagine that, Little Billie Briar Hopper, night club singer!

Well, it was just wonderful! I loved it!!!! I loved the music, music was so good then. I loved the people and they seemed to love me. I loved the waiters, and King, the head waiter, and Henry, the owner. Everybody was so nice to me.

Jimmy and I used to sing some duets; he taught me lots of songs. I grew to like a completely new kind of music; Jimmy said I was a natural jazz singer and "song stylist." I loved music so much, and I loved doing it my way. I phrased the way I felt, and they liked it!

Sometimes, a name band would play a dance out at the beach at Lumina, and when they got through for the night, they would come to the Plantation. Then we would have a jam session and nothing is better than that.

We had really top notch musicians at the Plantation, and this was a 14 piece orchestra. Charlie Friar came from WBT in Charlotte, he was a wonderful piano player, and then Gibb Young, and he was on the show with me for years in Charlotte and was the best guitar player I've ever heard. We had so many, really good, musicians, and I loved being a part of it all.

Life was good then. It was wonderful to be able to sleep as late as I wanted. When I'd wake up, Mama would have this wonderful "brunch", and we'd sit at the table for hours, talking about what a good time I'd had the night before. Then I'd go down town and meet Ann at Saunders Drug Store for an ice cream soda. Sometimes Jimmy and Charlie and some other members in the band would be there. If a good movie was at the Bailey Theater we would all go together, and later we would go someplace to eat, or some days I'd go shopping for a new evening dress. Then I'd go home and have supper and get ready to go to work. Jimmy and Charlie would come by about eight thirty and off we'd go to the Plantation.

The minute I opened the door when I got home at night, Daddy would call me to bring him a glass of water. I knew he was just checking on me, but I didn't care. Daddy might drink, but I knew he would kill me if I did. It wasn't any temptation at all to me; besides even if I had wanted to drink, John Davis, my favorite waiter would not have let me. No matter where I was sitting he would come over and pick up my drink and smell it; he was so afraid somebody was going to put something in my drink, but I don't think they ever did. I couldn't imagine why anybody would want to change the way they felt, I still don't, but sad to say, I've found some of the best people on this earth do.

The Plantation Club was almost like a second home to me. I was there from the early spring of 1942 until the autumn of 1946. I was not there continually. During these intermittent breaks I had plenty to do.

Jimmy Jett had formed his own orchestra and had given up his job as Manager of the Club. He devoted his time exclusively to his band. I worked with his orchestra always while he was in Wilmington. We played tobacco warehouses, wedding receptions, etc., and the Ocean Forest Hotel in Myrtle Beach. Jimmy and I also had a radio program on the only radio station, WMFD, here in Wilmington

The Ocean Forest was a beautiful, very elegant place. I remember sitting on the band stand thinking that this must be the most beautiful place in the world. Myrtle Beach was a wonderful beach back then. Not at all like it is now. Most of the time, though, we were at the Plantation.

The Plantation was a very nice dinner club, very well appointed. A doorman admitted a select clientele. A dress code was strictly enforced. Delicious food was served by impeccably dressed black men attired in immaculate white jackets. King, the head waiter, was resplendent in tails. Good behavior was demanded of the patrons.

Stags were not allowed at the Plantation, except periodically when a new squadron of pilots came to Blumenthal Air Base. Their commanding officers would bring them to the Plantation. At first intermission I had to go and sit at the head of this long table and welcome them. I really didn't like this very much, because I had to strain my voice to make them hear me. To tell you the truth, I just really wasn't all that interested in meeting men. I knew someday the right one would come along, but I just didn't have time for them yet. I met a lot of Officers that way, though. I dated some of them, but I only had one night a week off, and it was much more fun, to me, to go over to Aunt Minnie's and do something with Ann and Mary Daniel. It suited me fine though, to just stay home. I loved to put records on the machine and lie down and read, and I loved just being home with Mama and Daddy. Kingsland was always off somewhere with her friends, but I had to be away so much at night that it was really a treat to me to be able to stay home.

In 1944 Jimmy took his band on the road. He asked me to go, but I said "no." Not that I didn't want to go, but something told me I'd better not. Besides that, Mama and Daddy said I couldn't. So I stayed at the Plantation.

We got another band; it was pretty good, but not as good as Jimmy's. And it wasn't as much fun.

In the fall of that year I went to New York for the first time. My cousin, Mary Daniel and her best friend were going, and I prevailed upon them to let Foy, my best friend and me tag along. My intent was to break into show business up there. I had a letter of introduction to one of the senior executives at NBC. He proved to be a very influential person to know, for he secured a wonderful agent for me, and he opened the door to many wonderful opportunities. Also, my relatives up there, the Burton girls (remember?) had married very well, and it was my good fortune that they cleared a path for me to some of the most interesting and powerful people, people who seemed to be very impressed with me. Because I was not yet 21, I was unable to find work in any of the nightclubs, but I was offered a part on Broadway, and I had many offers to model. The agent, Mr. Lipset, advised me to do that. He said it would give me a lot of poise, and then when I became 21 there would be many, many places for me to sing.

To make a long story short, it seemed so easy, there just wasn't that much of a challenge. Too, I was homesick, and I thought I could always go back so I came home and went back to the Plantation.

I wonder now, how different my life might have been, if I had taken advantage of just one of the opportunities offered me. We've all heard the expression, "easy come, easy go." How true this is. You don't miss the water 'til the well runs dry; you don't truly appreciate what you have until you don't have it anymore. Too, I might really have amounted to something, but wouldn't I have missed the one most important thing in my life? Maybe deep inside, I'm a Presbyterian, for I do believe that our lives are predestined to turn out like they do. The part of my life that brought the greatest joy is also responsible for my greatest grief.

So, we take the good with the bad, but I am so thankful for the good, so thankful for the memories, even though they're all I have now. And the biggest question in my life is WHY? I'll never understand.

And the War Goes On ♫

It seemed like the war went on forever. Several German submarines were spotted very close to our coast line. In fact, several bodies from a wrecked submarine washed up on our beaches. All homes and cottages on our ocean front were outfitted with shades and curtains that "blacked out" the light in case the enemy might be near by watching. A strict curfew was enforced. "Air raid alerts" were common place, and these were taken seriously, every block had its own air raid "warden." You could be fined, heavily, if you didn't take cover, immediately. I was almost caught out one night walking our little dog and barely made it home before the air raid warden saw me.

Stockings were almost impossible to find. This was because nylon was needed for parachutes. Stores were able to only get a few pairs, and believe me, they were at a premium.

Cigarettes were really hard to find. These were considered "necessities" for our service men.

People were forced to use margarine, because the amount of butter our ration books allowed was only about enough for one day. Butter and steak, even milk were all used to feed our armed services.

Men between the ages of 18 and 40 all but disappeared; they were all off somewhere fighting this war. Many of these boys and men never made it home again. Even lots of women entered the service. Our world was filled with men and women in uniform. Television was non existent then, but every time we went to the movies we were able to see, first hand, what was going on in the movie news. This was almost like watching the six thirty national television news today. Radio, of course, kept us abreast of what was going on, as well.

Mary Daniel was going to San Francisco! She had gotten a job out there and they were paying her way. Ann had decided to go with her. Well, this idea appealed to me VERY much. I wanted to go too. Ever since I saw that movie, "Hello, Frisco, Hello" I had really wanted to go. Of course, Daddy said "no." Aunt Minnie, though, had sort of talked Mama into the idea. She said that because I hadn't been to college, this would be an education, of sorts, to me; that travel broadens one.

Daddy was vehement about this. I was not going and that was that. He said if I did go, I could never come back home again. Well, I was almost 21 years old, and I WAS going. Ann and Mary Daniel already had reservations on the train, but the earliest reservation I could get was a whole month away. Public transportation was used to transport our service men and women, and the first priority always went to them. I made my reservation, though, and set about saving money for my trip. Daddy refused to give me a dime. I even sold my record player.

The big day arrived. My train left at 7:30 P M. Aunt Minnie came out to take me to the depot. Foy was there too, to see me off. Daddy was furious! For the first time in my life I was defying him. Anyway, he fussed with Aunt Minnie, and he fussed with Mama, and he really was mad with me. Mama and Aunt Minnie were trying to placate him. All of a sudden Kingsland just collapsed in a dead faint. Then everybody was so concerned about her they forgot about me, and Aunt Minnie and Foy and I ran out and got in the car and went to the station. Before I got on the train I called home and Mama said Kingsland was fine. Kingsland had married a year earlier and was expecting a baby. She had come back home for the duration of the war because Howard, her husband, was in the navy, somewhere in the South Pacific. Anyway, they thought the baby was coming, and they were taking her to the hospital.

There were several people at the station to wish me "Bon Voyage" with flowers and candy and magazines to read. This was a long journey in those days, and here I was, by myself, going all the way across the United States. I was so excited! (And a little bit apprehensive.) Very soon after I boarded the train the porter came and made up my berth, and I went to bed. I couldn't sleep very much that night. I was worried about Kingsland and I was also kind of sad to think that I could never go back home again. (I was already sort of homesick.)

The next morning we were in Washington, DC, and I had to change trains. It was the 24th of March and the cherry trees were in bloom. They were so beautiful! I tried to call home, but nobody answered. I supposed they were all at the hospital.

The next leg of my journey would take me to Chicago where I'd have to change trains again. That second night I was already in my berth, rolling up my hair, when the conductor came through our car announcing that we were in Pittsburgh, Pa. The next thing I heard was somebody from Western Union calling my name. My heart almost stopped beating, but I stuck my head through the curtain and identified myself. He handed me a telegram. I could hardly bring myself to open it, I was so frightened. Anyway, I did open it, and it said: "Kingsland gave birth to 8 pound girl. Have a good time, and hurry home. Love, Daddy." Well, then I just broke down and cried, and I just wanted to go back home right then.

The next day when the train got to Chicago, I had to change train stations. So I got a taxi to take me to another depot. I put my bags in a locker, because I had a four hour wait. I went up to the ticket window to find out exactly what time I could board my train and would you believe, I was at the wrong station. I was so mad, (and kinda scared) for I had heard about all the gangsters in Chicago.

Anyway, I finally got to the right station, and when I got on the next train, The Rio Grande Flyer, I didn't have to change anymore. I was on that train for three days, and I met the nicest people. One man, a Captain in the Army, would come, every meal time, and take me to the dining car, and he'd pay for my meal, too. Any of you who can remember train travel, must surely remember the wonderful food in the dining car. It was like dining in the finest restaurant imaginable.

I got to know nearly everybody in my car, and they were all just wonderful to me. This was sort of a tourist travel train. There was a travel director who would point out places of interest. The train stopped for four hours in Denver and a whole crowd of us got off and went to a famous restaurant and to a movie.

When we crossed the Great Salt Lake in Utah the travel director explained a lot about that. Then we went through this long, long tunnel, right through a huge mountain. When we passed Reno, Nevada, it was snowing. The train stopped long enough for all of us (who wanted) to get off and have a snow ball fight. Then that last morning when I opened my eyes we were going through a beautiful orange grove, and our next stop was Oakland, California.

Oakland was as far as the train went. From there all passengers bound for San Francisco had to get on a ferry that would take them across the bay to San Francisco.

I remember kind of worrying....... what on earth I would do if Ann or Mary Daniel were not there to meet me. I didn't even know where they lived, and I didn't have very much money either.

Anyway, as the ferry neared San Francisco, I saw somebody standing on a baggage cart, waving as hard as they could, and it was my cousin, Ann. I was so relieved, and so happy. She said we weren't going to the place they lived right then, but that I was going back to work with her, that her boss wanted to meet me. Well, I told her that the first thing I had to do was get a new pair of shoes. (I had my ration book.) I didn't have very much money, and I spent most of that on those shoes. Then I went back to work with her and met her boss.

Sweetheart of the Carolinas

I took the long Civil Service test that very afternoon. They graded it immediately and told me to come to work the next morning. They put me in the typist pool. The only trouble was, I was not a good typist, (at all.) To make matters worse, Mary Daniel had been asking for an assistant, and guess who they made her assistant? Me! She was horrified! They told her I had made an unusually high score on my test, and they were sure I could learn anything I needed to know. They sent me to typing school every morning, but I never did become a good typist. We were having fun, though.

San Francisco 1945

San Francisco was a magical place in those days. It truly was not like any other place in this world. Of every place I've ever been San Francisco stands out as the best. Never have I ever felt so welcome, so admired.

We lived in a girl's residence hotel, The Florence. If you were fortunate enough to live there you had to adhere to very strict rules. We were only about two blocks from the top of Nob Hill, and only three blocks from the Mark Hopkins. We all three shared a room. There was a big Murphy bed, which Ann and I shared, and a day bed, which was Mary Daniel's. When you put the bed up and turned it around there was a huge full length mirror and behind that a very large closet. We also had a large bathroom. It was very, very nice, and we enjoyed living there. We really couldn't afford it, though.

We all three worked for the Army Ordinance Depot, and payday was once a month, and it was hard to stretch our money that long. We had to eat out every meal. San Francisco in conducive to good appetites, because it's always almost cold, and everywhere you go you either have to go up a hill or down a hill, and all that exercise makes you hungry.

Mary Daniel always had something for us to do. She wanted to see everything. Ann and I would get so tired, and we liked to go to movies more than "sight see."

Mary Daniel was always mad with me. She said I was the worst assistant imaginable, that every time she needed me I was in the rest room singing for the other employees. Well, you know how I like to sing.

Billie Holiday was appearing at the Savoy Club, and I absolutely had to see her, so I made them go with me. Well, we spent our last dime, but it was worth it. She was so wonderful! While we were watching her show, we met some boys who wanted to take us to the Top of the Mark. Well, we went, they were very nice, and we had a good time. The next morning I decided not to go to work. I was so sleepy, besides seeing Billie Holiday reminded me that the only thing I wanted to do was sing. Mary Daniel was really mad, she said she was gonna tell our boss so I'd get fired.

I stayed in bed until the nurse came. (When you worked for the government they always sent a nurse to check on you.)

As soon as the nurse left I got up and really dressed up, and started going around to the booking agents listed in the phone book. Well, the first one I saw told me to go to this place called "Diamond Lil's Palace" that night, and he'd meet me there, and I could audition. Ann and Mary Daniel went with me, and guess what? I couldn't believe it! It was part of the Savoy Club. I got the job, and then we had plenty of money.

I enjoyed singing at this place very much. There were these black handle bar mustaches on every table, and the whole decor was in the "gay nineties" style. Some nights I'd put on this big, black hat with lots of plumes on it and dress up like "Diamond Lil." It was so much fun. Everybody called me "Honey chile." I declare, they acted like they'd never seen a southerner before. They really teased me; the bartender asked me if North Carolina was in the United States.

The only trouble was that I couldn't quit my job with the government, because I was "frozen" to my job because of the war. Well, it was really hard for me to have to wake up and go to work after I'd been singing the night before. Finally though, they "thawed" me out and let me go.

One afternoon, before I was "thawed" out, I met Ann and Mary Daniel in the break room and every body in the whole room were crying. They had just announced that Roosevelt was dead. They let us go home immediately. The whole town closed up. There were no clubs or restaurants open in the whole town.

We got on the streetcar and went out to the beach and finally found a place to eat supper.

I could hardly believe that I was here so close to Billie Holiday! And even more unbelievable, she came in to hear me sing every night! She invited me to come to her dressing room during intermissions, and I really got to know her well. I saw her biography on television not long ago, and it was horrible! She was not at all like that. It makes me so mad, the way she is portrayed now. And she was beautiful. When she sang she reminded me of a golden statue, she hardly moved, and you, honestly, could hear a pin drop. She had that effect on people. I never heard her say a bad word or tell a dirty joke. She was just as nice as she could be. In fact, she reminded me a lot of Rosalie. She told everybody that I was her "baby." She loved to hear me sing "Georgia on My Mind." Every night she'd ask me to sing it. But she told me too, that she hated to see me get mixed up in the business, that she was sure I could make it, but that I wasn't the type, and she wanted me to go home and marry some nice, southern boy. She was really a good friend to me. I loved her dearly.

Every night Ann and Mary Daniel would come to the club to walk home with me, our hotel was only about four blocks away, and every night some boys would ask me to go out to eat. I always told them I couldn't go unless my cousins went, too. They were always more than glad to invite them. So, we'd all go to our favorite restaurant, which was just around the corner from our hotel, and every night I would order the same thing, two salads, and charcoal broiled fillet mignon. Mary Daniel said I was a "steak digger," because I'd make them order a steak, too. Mary Daniel said it was terrible to make those boys spend so much money, but I thought it was better for them to spend it on food than to waste it on alcohol. Besides, they didn't seem to mind, and most of them came back. We had a wonderful excuse for not inviting them in when we got to our hotel. Men were not allowed to enter the building after 9 p. m., and they were never allowed beyond the sitting room, no matter what time it was.

On the way to work at night I'd stop by the B and G Grill, which was in the same block as the Savoy, they served the best Welsh rarebit I've ever tasted. I gained 20 pounds in no time at all. That was good; I'd always wanted to gain weight.

The San Francisco Conference was going on. That was the beginning of United Nations.

There were millions of foreigners every where and the town was running over with celebrities. It was very exciting. Ann and Mary Daniel used to go and sit in the lobby of the St.

Francis Hotel, just to see who might be coming in or going out. I couldn't go because I was always singing, but I saw my share of them, anyway. They were everywhere.

This sheik and his entourage began to come in every night. They would always occupy the very first table. He had a mouth full of gold teeth, and he would just sit there grinning like an idiot. I don't think he could speak a word of English. I don't know why he came to hear me sing, because I doubt if he could understand any of my songs. Anyway, one night, one of the men at his table asked if he could speak to me, and do you know what he said? He said that man wanted to take me home with him, to be in his harem, I suppose. Well, I was speechless! I told him, "Certainly not." Can you imagine the pure gall of some people? After a while they stopped coming, and I was very relieved.

Really and truly, though, something exciting was always happening. I really felt guilty because I wasn't any more homesick than I was, so I always wrote Mama and Daddy sad letters so they would think I missed them a lot. Well, I really did, but just not as much as I thought I should.

One night soon after I got to work this group of Navy men came in. There were four of them, and they seemed exceptionally nice, and they were all very nice looking. They had just come into port after having been out to sea for many months and were looking forward to going home on leave the next day. They started talking to me, and I found out that they were all four from the south; I suppose that was why, right off the bat, we seemed to have such a good rapport. They stayed until closing time, and they took Ann and Mary Daniel and me to the steak place that night.

You know how sometimes you meet people, and it's almost like you've known them forever. Well, that's how it was.

Well, about two weeks later, one of them came back. His name was Jimmy Jemison. He was the one I had really gotten to know best. He had told me he was a medical student at Tulane and was studying to be a doctor, but had volunteered for naval service when the war started. He really was very, very nice, and I really did like him a lot. He was from New Orleans, and he knew a lot about music. I could tell he came from a very nice family, and he had beautiful manners.

Anyway, he said he had come back early, because he wanted to get to know me better. Later, when Ann and Mary Daniel came they were so glad to see him, Ann had told me he was coming back; she said she just had a feeling. I hadn't even practiced my hypnotism on him; to tell you the truth, there didn't seem to be much point. After that he came every night for the rest of his leave. Ann and Mary Daniel were crazy about him. When his friends came back all four of them came as often as they could. Soon after that four Naval Officers came in. They told me they were from Jimmy's ship, that they had heard so much about me and they wanted me to be their ship's mascot.

I knew Jimmy was going to ask me to marry him, and I decided I would. After all, I was 21, and I supposed it was time. He really didn't look, at all, like I had imagined he would, but he was very nice looking. Too, I thought it would be nice when I went back home to be engaged. That way I wouldn't have to date so much. Maybe my 'prince charming' was all in my head and didn't exist.

Daddy wrote to me often, about his garden and about how much they missed me. Mama wrote about how cute Susan, Kingsland's baby, was and I really did want to see her. Ann was ready to go home because the war in Europe was over and Bobby was coming home. To tell the truth, I was beginning to be homesick. I was having the best time I had ever had in my life, but I wanted to go home. Mary Daniel thought I was crazy, because she couldn't understand why I would want to leave when I was having such a wonderful time. Our "house mother", the lady who owned our hotel, said she knew I could get in the movies if I stayed out there.

Jimmy, the boy I had promised to marry, begged me to marry him before I went home, but I told him I couldn't possibly do that, that I had to tell my parents, in person, first, and that I knew they wouldn't let me even think about getting married until the war was completely over.

Ann answered an ad in the paper. It seemed this woman was driving back to Virginia, and she was looking for some people to go with her. She would charge just sixty dollars a piece. Of course, we'd have to pay for our food and our motels along the way. She wanted to go by Yosemite and the Grande Canyon and other places of interest, and it really sounded like a wonderful trip, so we decided to go with her.

Mary Daniel said we were crazy to even think about going on a trip like that with somebody we didn't know, but she seemed like a very nice lady. Mary Daniel didn't want to go home yet; she had written to a friend in Wilmington, whose fiancée had been killed in the war, and had convinced her to come to San Francisco, so it wasn't like we were leaving her out there by herself.

I really hated to leave the place I was working. The people who worked there were so nice to me. Billie Holiday had already left, but Art Tatum was there and Chi Chi Rose Murphy. They all dedicated the whole night to me, and I got lots of presents. Syd Fox and Lou Wolfe, the owners of the club, (I thought that was so funny, Fox and Wolfe) said I could come back anytime I wanted. So I told them all good bye.

Jimmy walked me back to the hotel. He really didn't want me to go. He said if I would just reconsider, that we could go to Las Vegas that very night and get married, and then if I was determined to go home, he'd buy me a plane ticket. We walked around the block three or four times, while he was trying to convince me. The only thing I could do was to ask him to let me think about it seriously that night, and I'd decide the next day.

Well, the next morning, early, Ann and I got up and took a taxi over the bridge to Oakland and met Mrs. Sardini, and started on our long journey home. Mary Daniel said we hadn't been gone 15 minutes when Jimmy came, that he just broke down and cried like a baby when she told him we had left. She said she felt so sorry for him, that he really was so disappointed.

It was Saturday and she didn't have to work so she spent the day with him trying to console him. I felt guilty too, leaving like I did, but I just wasn't ready to get married.

It turned out to be the most wonderful trip. There was another woman who was older than we were; she was married. Her husband had shipped out. She was going to have a baby and was going home to her family in Norfolk, Va. There was also a man who was about 30 I guess and of course, Mrs. Sardini. She was real old, about 40 I think.

We just had the best time in the world and we zig zagged all over the United States going to all these interesting places. Mrs. Sardini and the other woman, Ruth, shared a room and they always went to bed early. Ann and I shared a room, and the man, Paul, stayed by himself. After the others had gone to bed he would take Ann and me out, so we got to see a lot of the local life everywhere we went.

They all took turns driving except me, because I didn't know how to drive, and everybody took turns sitting in the front seat, including me. That made Ann mad because she said that since I didn't drive, I shouldn't sit in the front seat. That was the only disagreement we had. The reason everybody wanted to sit in the front seat was because it was so much cooler than the back seat. Cars weren't air conditioned then.

It was so hot! This was before air conditioning, and going through Arizona and New Mexico the heat was almost unbearable. When we'd stop to eat, the water they would serve us was just as hot as the air. Some days we would sleep in the day time and drive at night. Some of the motels were air conditioned, if not, at least there was a fan. Other than that, it was a wonderful trip. We spent a night and day in Yosemite. Stopped at Boulder Dam, spent a night and day at the Grand Canyon. We went through Las Vegas. It was just a small town then, the only really nice motel was the Last Frontier, (or was it the Lost Frontier?) and we had breakfast there. We just zig zagged up and down across the USA. It took us almost two weeks, but we enjoyed every minute.

Every night, after Ann had gone to sleep, I would go in the bathroom, (so I wouldn't have to disturb Ann by leaving the light on) and write to Jimmy, every single night. I really did feel sort of guilty.

Finally, we got as far as Charlotte, which was as close as Mrs. Sardini would get to Wilmington. We had a few hours before our bus left for Wilmington, and I wanted to go up to WBT and see the people that I had grown up with. Well, we had nearly gotten to the Wilder Building when who should we see walking down the street but Charlie, (remember?) the piano player at the Plantation? This really is a small world. Then we went up to the sixth floor of the Wilder Building, (where the studios of WBT were located) and saw everybody, and of course I had to sing on the program. It was so much fun. Then it was time for our bus to leave and we were on the last leg of our journey home.

How wonderful to be home again, and Kingsland's baby was so cute. I was just so glad to see everybody.

The next day Mama and I were uptown shopping, when who should I see but Henry, the owner of the Plantation. I hadn't even called to tell him I was home and hadn't planned to call for at least a week... He seemed very glad to see me and wanted to know when I was coming back to work. I asked when he would need me and he said "tonight." Well, I really didn't want to go back so soon. I had so much to talk to Mama about, and besides my aunt Allene, Gideon's wife, was in town visiting Aunt Minnie, and she and her little girl and little boy were coming over that afternoon. I loved my little cousins, and I enjoyed telling them stories and had planned to take them to the park. I didn't know how long they would be in town, and I wanted to spend some time with them. So I asked Henry if I could just wait 'til that weekend, which seemed to be agreeable with him. Gideon, my uncle, was in the army over in Europe somewhere, and we were all concerned about him.

Anyway, I went back to the Plantation that Saturday night. It was a totally different band. I knew the leader, Virgil West, because he had played in Jimmy Jett's band. He had a woman pianist who played beautifully, but she couldn't transpose at all. I had to sing everything in the original key which meant I had to use my "high" voice. I sang mostly show tunes, because they were the ones she knew. I couldn't sing "my" songs; Mean to Me, Old Rocking Chair and Basin Street Blues, Georgia, etc. It really was different, because I loved singing the songs I loved, and singing them the way they felt. That, to me, is what music is all about. More than just singing a song, you're telling a story, the way it feels to you.

It was good to be back, though, as I've said before, the Plantation was my second home. One night, and this was the first week after I got back, my life was to change forever.

I was sitting on the bandstand, listening to the music, smiling, watching the dancers, when all of a sudden; I couldn't believe it, THERE HE WAS! He was dancing with a girl I had seen lots of times, because she came to the club often. Well, I couldn't breathe! I held my breath 'til he turned around, I had to see his face, and it was HIM!!!!! Here he was the one I had dreamed about all these years. My chair was always next to the piano on the bandstand, and I turned to the piano player and told her that THERE was the man I was gonna marry. I mean I started hypnotizing him right away and just as hard as I could. It was almost like a dream, here was the 'prince charming' I had pictured when I was a little girl, the one that appeared in all the fairy tales that I had read. He DID exist, there he was! HERE he was!

He came back the next night with the same girl. At intermission I was talking to the hat check girl, when who should come walking by but HIM! He told me that he certainly did enjoy my singing He also told me he was from Texas and that he owned a club in Houston and would be honored if I would consider singing there. He said he'd like to talk to me about it and wondered if I would speak to the doorman and have it arranged so that he could come in by himself some night. Then he introduced himself, said his name was Bob Daniel and that he trusted that we'd be seeing a lot of each other in the future. I told him that my grandmother's maiden name was Daniel and that we might be cousins. Really though, there just aren't that many Daniels that don't have an s on the end. Well, as soon as he went back to his table, I went into the hat check room and wrote "Billie Daniel" on the wall, and then I went to the main entrance and told Whit, the doorman, to let him in when he came back.

I told Mama about him while we were having brunch the next day, and tears came in her eyes. She asked me what I was going to do about Jimmy, and do you know, I had forgotten about him. I just couldn't think about him anymore that was all. This was the way it was meant to be. I knew it.

Well, that was the beginning, but that was the ending too of my life as a self confident, lucky little girl, who up until that time had somehow been granted every thing I desired; who took good fortune in stride, and who had never even wondered why, why was I so lucky?

Bob was in the Marine Corps, he was not a commissioned officer, but his uniforms were tailor made and tailored beautifully, and his bearing was such that he looked like he should be a young General. He was stationed in Camp Le Jeune, which was about 50 miles from Wilmington, so it took him a while just to go and come, but he came back the next night. He seemed perfectly content to wait around while I was on the bandstand. During intermissions he would come and escort me to his table. His manners were beautiful, everything about him was beautiful. He was very interesting, very "with it." He appeared to be a perfect gentleman in every way. He came back every night, and even before our first date I had fallen "head over heels."

The night of our first date I could hardly wait for the time for him to come, so Mama could meet him. Dora, our cleaning woman, stayed late so she could meet him. Everybody

118

was excited, because I had been so completely "not" interested in boys before that.

Well, he was late! Finally, he got there, he'd been held up in traffic or something, I can't remember now, but Mama said just watching me, so anxiously waiting for him, she just had a premonition that my carefree days were over, and it broke her heart. And you know she was right. My life was never the same after that.

If you're thinking, "what a foolish girl" well, I'll agree. It just never occurred to me that some things are more important than looks and polish and first impressions. And it never occurred to me, either, that some day things wouldn't come as easy for me; that some day, my life would take a turn. But even if I had known, if I could have, somehow, seen the heartache, the deprivation, the despair that lay ahead, would I have taken the same path? The answer is "yes." Yes, yes, yes, a million times, yes! For all the pain that I've endured, the joy that was mine far exceeded that pain.

I'm getting ahead of my story; now I'll get back to Bob. He asked me to marry him on that first date; he didn't get down on his knees or anything like that. What he said was, "If I asked you to marry me, what would you say," and with no hesitation at all, I said, "yes." After that he came to the Plantation every night, and on the weekends he'd come and spend the days with us. Mama liked him a lot, and he liked her, too. More and more, though, I began to sense that the people at work didn't care for him. I couldn't understand why.

I hadn't heard from Jimmy Jemison for over a month, and every day I didn't get a letter I was relieved. I hoped that, maybe, he'd changed his mind; I didn't know how to tell him that I had. He was so nice, I really liked him, but I was just not in love with him. Then one day, the mail man brought me thirty six letters from him. He'd been out at sea and had written every day, but couldn't mail anything until he reached some port. I hate to admit it, but I didn't even read all those letters. I've done a lot of things for which I am ashamed. Maybe I deserved a lot of the trouble that came my way, but is there anything bad enough that I could have done that would make me deserve the worst thing that could ever happen to me? And the worst thing that could ever happen did happen.

None of us knew it, of course, but VJ (victory in Japan) day was very near. We'd heard smatterings about an atom bomb that was being developed. Then one day the radio was filled with Hiroshima and the 'a' bomb that we had exploded there. I wrote in my diary that day, "the world is waiting, waiting for this seemingly endless war to end." Late that afternoon we got the news. IT was finally over! The world exploded with joy, it was over!

All service men were confined to base, but when I got to the Plantation that night I was greeted at the door by several Marine Corps officers that I knew. I'm sure they were AWOL, but I suppose they were excused. Anyway, Whit, the doorman, had let them in. I think there were exceptions for everything that night. They were waiting for me to get there, because I had promised everybody that the day the war ended I would have a REAL drink with them. They had a bottle of Sparkling Burgundy cooling on the bar, and I had my first taste. I liked it very much.

And so the war was over, but the next night when Bob came he told me he was being transferred to Great Lakes, Michigan. I really did miss him after he left. He wrote, but not every day. I began to wonder if he loved me as much as I loved him. And the people at the Plantation seemed to be so glad that he was gone. They didn't like him it all and I couldn't understand. I got so mad that finally I just quit. Henry and Gay, his wife, kept asking me to come back, but I was really mad with all of them. I hadn't heard from Bob for weeks, so I supposed he'd met somebody else, and I was ashamed to go back to the Plantation and tell them that they'd been right about him. So I decided to go back to Charlotte.

Mama and Daddy didn't argue with me, they wanted me to forget about Bob, too, I'm sure.

I didn't even bother to tell Clarence I was coming. I just packed my bags and got on the bus and was there.

I went straight up to WBT and told Carolyn Fraley the receptionist that I wanted to surprise Clarence. She rang his office and told him that he had to come out to the front desk immediately. He must have asked her "why?" because she said "Please, Mr. Etters, I don't have time to answer questions, just please get out here as fast as you can." (Carolyn was a good friend of mine and of Clarence, too.) She was also a prankster, and loved to play jokes on people.

Well, he seemed delighted to see me, but when I told him I was there to stay he looked a little chagrined. I'm sure he didn't know what to do with me. You see, the war had just recently ended. The world was just beginning to get back to normal. There were no vacant apartments, no rooms for rent; there was no place for me to stay. He called this woman he knew who had a large boarding house for girls, and asked her if she possibly had a vacancy. She didn't, she said there were no vacancies anywhere in town. Anyway, he invited her to go out to dinner with us. She accepted, and we went by to pick her up.

Her name was Mrs. Thomas, Aileen Thomas, and she was just lovely! Right off the bat, I was just crazy about her. She was so pretty, had the prettiest silver hair, and wore the most beautiful clothes. She reminded me a lot of Aunt Fanny, if Aunt Fanny had worn a lot of make up. She told me she was 53, and I remember thinking how could anybody be so pretty and be so old.

After we had eaten, Clarence took us up to the Variety Club, and we talked for hours. She had a daughter who was 27. She was a singer too, and was working in a cocktail lounge in Miami. She said her daughter used to come up to WBT to hear me sing, that she thought I was very talented.

To make a long story short, she liked me so much that she invited me to come and stay with her in her private suite, in her daughter's room. (Which I think Clarence was hoping she would do.)

Well, I absolutely loved living with Mrs. Thomas. It was a beautiful, huge old home called Royal Oaks, and there were 20 girls living there, and they were very nice girls; (Mrs. Thomas wouldn't have them, if they weren't.) She had a wonderful cook and served delicious food. We ate with the girls, and I got to know them all. Mrs. Thomas loved music and had a piano in our quarters, which she played beautifully. She also had the best record collection that I had ever seen. She loved my "high" voice and told Clarence that I should be groomed for musical comedy. We were completely compatible, she was another one of those people you meet sometimes, and it's like you've known them forever. She reminded me, so much, of my great aunts that I adored.

The only meal she served on Sunday was breakfast and I loved going out with the girls to eat. I made some good friends, one in particular whose name was Melanie. I introduced her to her future husband.

Clarence went to lunch nearly every day at the S and W Cafeteria. The S&W was like no other cafeteria I've ever known. The food was delicious. Frank Sherrill, the owner, was a good friend of his. Some of the women who worked at WBT would usually go with him, and I'd always go, too.

Clarence and another man, Johnny Matthews, had an orchestra together. It was considered to be the best one in Charlotte, and everything about it was wonderful. The first Saturday I was there he introduced me to his partner and I sang for him. After that I became the vocalist with their band. We played at the Charlotte Country Club or the Myers Park Club nearly every weekend. Sometimes we'd go to the Carolina Hotel in Pinehurst, sometimes the main Officers Club at Ft.

Bragg. We stayed pretty busy. I loved the band. Clarence also got me a job selling records in a music store. I really enjoyed that job, because I got to learn all the newest songs the minute they came out.

Charlotte's baseball team then was called the Charlotte Hornets. Some of the players used to come in to buy records, and I got to know them. After a while all of them came in and they asked me to be the mascot of their club. That was fun. I dated one of them, he had the bluest eyes I've ever seen, and I liked him, but he was just a friend. We double dated with a good friend of his; I introduced him to my friend, Melanie. It was love at first sight, I think. Anyway, they were married about a year later.

Clarence and Mrs. Thomas got their heads together, and decided, definitely, that I be groomed for musical comedy. I wasn't all that enthused about it, but never-the-less Clarence took me out to Queens College and had me sing for Olive Maine, who was considered to be one of the finest voice teachers in the south. She very graciously accepted me as a student.

Clarence was delighted, so was Mrs. T. My life, it seemed, was gonna start moving in a different direction altogether, and I really liked it the way it was.

126

I Was So Happy! ♫

One day I went up to the broadcasting station to meet Clarence and he was in a meeting, so I sat down to wait. I don't know what prompted me to do it, but I borrowed some paper from Carolyn and started writing a letter to Bob. I still thought about him, still couldn't understand why I'd stopped hearing from him. Anyway, it was a very short letter. I just told him that I'd moved to Charlotte, that I was quite happy, (I was, really) and I was wondering how he was doing. Well, three or four days later, even before breakfast, the door bell rang, and guess what? There was a special delivery letter for me from Bob! I was so happy! He gave me his phone number and told me to call him collect just as soon as I got this letter. That's what I did. He asked for my phone number, and after that he called everyday. About a week later he told me he was coming. Well, I was probably the happiest person in the world. I couldn't wait to see him.

He arrived two days later. I had never seen him in a suit before. I'll never forget how handsome he looked.

I was so wonderfully happy to see him. It seemed so right to be with him. It was like I had known him forever. Bob was just not like anybody I had ever known before, and he seemed to understand me perfectly. I really thought he was the one meant for me, and that I was meant for him.

Maybe I still believed in fairy tales. I think when I look back now, that I was almost like a child still, even though I was 21 years old. Maybe being 'little Billie Briar hopper' all those years kept me a child, for everybody treated me as though I were a child. I really knew very little about love. I knew I loved him, though.

At first everybody was crazy about him, the girls at Royal Oaks thought he was the best looking thing they had ever seen. Clarence seemed to like him a lot. He ate lunch with all of us everyday. At night he'd take me out to dinner. When he brought me home we'd sit on the front porch and talk. Mrs. Thomas would come downstairs at eleven thirty and turn on the porch light and tell Bob it was time for me to come in, (they treated me just like I was a child) and he'd go back to his hotel. On the nights I had to sing he'd go with us. He was a perfect gentleman; I don't know why all of a sudden they started not liking him.

Then, after he'd been there about three weeks, Daddy called me at work one morning.

He told me that Mama was very sick and was going to have major surgery the next morning, and that I'd better come home as quickly as I could. Well, I just went all to pieces, you know how much I loved my mother, but I really hated to go off and leave Bob while he was there in Charlotte.

Bob went with me to the bus station. It seemed like everybody from WBT was there that afternoon. They said they were so sorry about Mama and for me not to worry, that they were sure she would be fine. Bob got on the bus with me and waited 'til time for it to leave; then he got off and we waved good-bye. When the bus pulled off Carolyn and Clarence and the girls who ate lunch with us everyday were all waving. Seemed as though they wanted to be sure I was on that bus.

After I left, you won't believe what they did, but I'll get to that later.

When I finally got to Wilmington nobody was there to meet me. It was in the middle of the night, and Daddy always met me no matter what time it was. I was scared to death that maybe Mama was dead. I got a taxi and rushed into the house. No lights were even on, I went straight to their room, and Mama and Daddy were in bed asleep! I screamed, "Mama!" and when they woke up they just started laughing. Laughing! Do you believe it? Mama wasn't even sick. Clarence had called her and told her to come to Charlotte, and she thought it would be better for me to just come home. So Daddy just made that up about her being sick. That was the only way they knew, for certain, to make me come. Oh, I was so mad! Have you ever heard of anything like that?

Mama said she asked Clarence what had Bob done that was so bad, (Mama really liked Bob), and he told her that they just didn't think he was right for me, that apparently he didn't have a job, and they were just afraid that we would run away and get married, and that someday when I did get married I needed to marry somebody who was more responsible than Bob appeared to be. Well, it took me a long time to forgive them for that.

And do you know what Clarence and those people from WBT did after I left? They had a private detective accost Bob and tell him to go back to Texas, that he was not welcome in Charlotte. Sounds like the wild west, doesn't it?

You know when I look back and think about this now it doesn't seem real, but this is just exactly the way it happened.

Well, I went back to Charlotte, but I was furious with Clarence and with Mrs. Thomas, too, cause I knew they were in this together. I certainly did not want to live with Mrs. Thomas anymore. I called this girl that Clarence dated some. She had told me just before I went home that she was looking for somebody to share her apartment. I moved in with her the first day I got back.

I still sang with Clarence's band, (it was really a wonderful orchestra) but I was extremely mad with him.

People really liked the way I sang back then, I had a lot of special arrangements and I loved to "swing" some of the semi classics. When I'd stand up to sing lots of people would stop dancing and they'd all come and stand around the band stand.

I stopped meeting Clarence and his "entourage" for lunch. Carolyn, though, kept calling me and apologizing, she said she went along with the rest of them because they all did it for my own good, that they loved me and thought I had such a bright future, and they were afraid I'd run away and marry Bob. And do you know what she asked me? She asked me if I had ever been "intimate" with Bob, and I told her "oh! Yes," that right from the very beginning I had always felt like I could tell him anything. Then it dawned on me that wasn't the kind of 'intimate' she meant. I could tell by the way she looked so shocked when I said "oh, yes." Then I figured Clarence had put her up to that, and I got mad with him all over again. I didn't stay mad with Carolyn though, I really loved her and her fiancée, too (they were married soon afterwards.) We remained friends for the rest of her life. Her life is another story, a sad story.

Bob called and Mrs. Thomas wouldn't give him my new number. All she told him was that I had moved, and she wouldn't tell him where. Finally he sent me a letter in care of WBT, and somebody in the mail room called me, and I went up there and got it. (It's just a good thing Clarence didn't find out about it until it was too late.) I probably never would have even known about it.

After that, Bob wrote often, but then after a while not quite so often. I just practically lived for his letters and when they stopped coming so often, I became completely disillusioned. I couldn't believe that this was happening again. I wondered, could everybody be right, was I just maybe an idiot to believe in him. And I certainly wouldn't tell them, maybe if they hadn't practically made him leave, he'd still be in Charlotte and we could have gotten married. I was just such a child. I never gave a thought to how we'd live if we did get married. Well, I thought I would always sing and make pretty good, and Bob was so good looking I knew he could get a good job. (He said we could live on the Pacific Ocean and dive for pearls, and I thought that would be fun too.)

It wasn't as much fun being in Charlotte after I got mad with Clarence and Mrs. Thomas. Clarence had been my very best friend in the world ever since I was twelve years old, and I couldn't believe that he was being so mean now.

One night out at the Myers Park Club during intermission the whole band was sitting at a big table. I was at the head of the table, Clarence was my left and Johnny, his partner, was on my right. They started talking to me, saying what a brilliant future I had, and that they wanted me to forget about Bob, that he was just not right for me; that someday I'd marry some rich man who could lavish everything on me that my heart desired. They just couldn't understand that the only thing my heart desired was Bob.

I was really like the song says, "between the devil and the deep blue sea." I was mad with everybody in Charlotte and with everybody in Wilmington. Mama and Daddy wanted me to come home, so I decided to go on back to Wilmington, anyway.

My friend Foy had gone back to her home in a little town close to Bixby, NC, and had been urging me to come to see her, so since she lived sort of between Charlotte and Wilmington I decided to visit her for a while. She was one of the few people in the world I wasn't mad with then, and I loved her whole family dearly. I was just crazy about her big brothers. Well, I just had the best time in the world! Her mother was this wonderful, crazy lady who was the Mayor of the town. She had put signs up all over every where saying that little Billie Briar Hopper was coming, and she had gotten this great big truck from somewhere and had it parked in her front yard, and all these people came from all over the country side. I had to go up on a tall ladder and get on top of this truck and stand up there (with no music) and sing. Then she had all kinds of refreshments for everybody, and it was the most fun. I really did enjoy that visit.

When I got back to Wilmington I didn't let anybody at the Plantation know I was back.

There was an ad in the paper for somebody to announce and play records. I went down and applied and got the job. It was something new they were trying. Instead of having "juke boxes" in every restaurant, they had speakers in every booth. I was in a little studio with a microphone and two turntables. I would announce what I was gonna play and play the record, if the people in the booth wanted to hear it they'd put a nickel in the slot and then the music would be piped into that booth. Well, it was fun at first, but I got a lot of complaints because I would just play what I wanted to hear. It didn't take long to get tired of that job, I'll tell you.

Anyway, I finally got my nerve up and called Henry, and he said to come on back; he promised they wouldn't tease me or say anything bad about Bob so I went back to the Plantation.

It was good to be back and to see everybody. I was really very fond of some of our regular customers. Most of them were married older couples who'd been coming weekly, sometimes two or three times a week ever since I'd been singing out there. They were all so nice to me. Some of them were couples that I had watched fall in love, right before my eyes, as they danced the night away to the music of Jimmy Jett's orchestra, couples who had danced their last dance together, before the Soldier or the Marine was shipped over seas, and who had somehow returned, unscathed, to be reunited once again at the Plantation. (Many of them were not so lucky.)

I was very fond of the people who worked out there, too. It was good to be back.

Bob's letters became few and far between. He called me sometimes at the Plantation, but never at home. He sent a telegram once saying he was leaving Texas that night, driving to Wilmington. I was so happy, I told everybody, but he never got there. Henry asked me several days later if he was coming by mule train. I didn't even get mad with him. By then I'd just about given up on Bob.

My cousin Hattie had moved to Wilmington to work for the Atlantic Coast Line. We double dated a lot on my nights off. I met lots of Wilmington boys that had come home from the service. I hadn't known them before. I wasn't very happy, though. No matter how I tried I couldn't stop thinking about Bob.

I had been back at the Plantation three or four months when out of a clear blue sky Charlie Friar (remember? From Jimmy Jetts' band?) called. He was working at Andy's Supper Club over in Fayetteville and the owner of the club was interested in me. Why didn't I take the weekend off and come over to Fayetteville and let him see me and sing for him? He said he thought I'd love it over there.

So that's what I did. Charlie had a room with this lady named Ruth Sandrock. She had a lot of money and a very nice home. She invited me to stay with her that weekend; she had a lovely hone and lots of room and just loved music and musical people. Her ex son-in-law was the owner of the club, and she was still very friendly with him. Mrs. Sandrock was 68 years old. They say her husband was really tight; he had all this money but was almost a miser. Well, after Mr. Sandrock died, Mrs. Sandrock worked very hard spending his money.

Jimmy Norman, the owner hired me on the spot, and Mrs. Sandrock invited me to live with her. I'll tell you the truth; she was almost like a fairy god mother. She had the best cook in the world and she'd let Charlie and me decide what we wanted to have for dinner every night. She had all my clothes washed and ironed and twice a week she'd have a fresh box of chocolate candy by my bed, and fresh flowers in my room. She let me buy all the records I wanted and charge them to her. She loved to dance, would come out to Andy's several times a week and bring a big crowd with her and would buy steaks and Champaign for everybody.

I loved living with her and I loved singing at Andy's. Andy's was nothing like the Plantation; it was much less formal. I didn't even wear evening dresses except on weekends, and the men in the band didn't wear uniforms, just nice suits. It wasn't even an orchestra really, but a small combo that was very good. (I really enjoyed singing more with small combos than with a big band.) Charlie, of course, played the piano, and he was wonderful; I could sing all my songs. The saxophone player had been in Jimmy Jett's band, and he was the best. There was a wonderful trumpet man and a drummer and a clarinet. The food was really good, but not served as elegantly. Stags were allowed. Most of them were Officers from Fort Bragg. Some Fayetteville people, of course, but it was really like a glorified Officers Club.

Jimmy Norman, the owner and his wife, Becky, were there every night. She was a delightful, beautiful, tiny little person, always exuberant and fun to be around. His sister Carol worked there, too.

Charlie and I double dated a lot on our nights off. We loved to go out to the main Officer's Club. Down in the basement (they called it the Cess pool) it was almost like Reno or Las Vegas. You never saw so many slot machines. Sometimes we'd go out there in the afternoon. They let us go to the PX anytime we wanted, too.

One of the regulars, who came every Sunday night, was a Mr. Smith from Pinehurst. They called him Smitty. He was a gambler and had a whole string of race horses. He never did say very much to me, but he'd always request a song. Then after I'd sung it, he'd come up to the bandstand and give me a twenty dollar bill, which I was supposed to split with the band. Then he'd give me another twenty which was all mine. On top of that at intermission, when I stepped down from the bandstand he'd be there and he'd ask me if I didn't want a steak. I nearly always said "yes" and when they'd bring the steak underneath it there would be a brand new twenty dollar bill. He never did sit at the table with me or anything; he would just send the steak. Mostly, he'd just stand around and talk to the owner of the club and Carol, the hat check girl (who was the owner's sister) and the doorman, and he never stayed very long, hardly ever more than an hour. Every Sunday night when he came in Carol would come up to the bandstand and tell me to look hungry, 'cause Smitty was here. One night he came in and said he'd just bought a race horse and he'd named it Billie Burton. I never heard about it winning any races, though.

Another regular was Capt. McCormick. I usually sat at his table during first intermission and had a cup of coffee. Everybody liked him. He'd always ask me to sing Brahms Lullaby, and I would every night. I liked Capt. McCormick a whole lot.

One night I was sitting on the bandstand, watching the dancers (deja vu) when all of a sudden, out there on the dance floor, I saw somebody who looked like Bob. Same build, same dark hair. When he turned around and I saw his face he didn't really look like Bob at all. He looked like Gregory Peck, (you can't get much better than that.) Anyway, after he and his date went back to their table, he went over and spoke to Capt.

McCormick. At the next intermission I went back over to Capt. McCormick's table and asked him who in the world he was. Well, Capt. McCormick started laughing. He said he was Lt. Ray Johnson, and that he had come over to his table to ask him to introduce me to him.

So I met him and gave him my phone number, and the next day he called me. After that he came nearly every night. If he had OD and couldn't come he'd send somebody to get me and take me out to his Officer's Club so I could eat supper with him, and then he'd send me to work. On the weekends he'd come and spend the day and we'd go to the movies, or just stay at Mrs. Sandrock's and listen to music and dance. (He was teaching me to dance because most of my life when I should have been dancing, I'd been on the band stand, and it was a rule I couldn't dance with the customers. If it wasn't a house rule, I'd make it one.) Anyway, I fell head over heels in love with him. Was it on the "rebound?" I don't know. I just know I loved him. The only trouble was he was engaged. He was engaged to a girl back home that he had known all his life and they were going to be married Christmas. So even though I knew it was hopeless I still couldn't wait to see him every night.

He was transferred to Ft. McClellan, Alabama in late November, and I never will forget that first day after he left. I

142

was just completely lost. I dreaded the thought of Christmas. I couldn't bear to think of him being married to somebody else.

Anyway, I kept singing, and I still enjoyed living at Mrs. Sandrocks. She was the best thing in the world to me. She couldn't wait for Christmas, so she gave me my Christmas present Thanksgiving night. (I think she felt sorry for me, she knew how much I missed my Lt.) Then she gave me another present every night 'til Christmas. She was something else, I'll tell you.

Christmas was drawing near. Charlie and I had a radio program on the local radio station to advertise the club. That was the first year I ever heard "I'll Be Home for Christmas," and I sang it a lot. It's funny, I can almost tell you what year it was, even now, if you'll tell me what songs were popular. Back then, though, there were so many good songs, and so many good singers. Peggy Lee was in her hey day, and nobody, before or since, has ever equaled her. That year "It's All Over Now" was probably her top seller. I can remember Charlie's songs, "Old Buttermilk Sky," and "I Love You for Sentimental Reasons." Oh, to be able to go back to those times, how lucky I was. How lucky to have these memories.

So many years have come and gone. So many things have happened, some so good, some so unbelievably horrendous. Still, I thank God for the good, but oh, how I wish some things could have been different.

He Was Back ♫

It was the week before Christmas. At first intermission I was sitting with Capt. McCormick as usual. I just happened to look up as the doorman opened the door, and there was Bob. At first, I couldn't believe it, and then, (Charlie said you could hear me all over the club) I screamed "BOB!!!!" I jumped up and ran to the door. He was back! I cannot possibly describe how I felt; I was just thrilled beyond words. I couldn't imagine how Bob even knew I was in Fayetteville, because I hadn't written to him since I'd been there. He said he had gone to Wilmington and called and Kingsland had told him where I was. (She didn't know it was him.)

Mr. Norman, the owner of the club, told me I could go on home, so that's what I did. I don't know if I've ever been happier in my life. When we got to Mrs. Sandrock's she could not have been nicer. She told Bob it would be silly for him to get a hotel room, that there were two beds in Charlie's room, and she insisted that he stay there.

Mrs. Sandrock was really smitten by Bob, but then most people were when they first knew him. His manners were impeccable. He knew exactly how to charm everybody, especially older people. I wish I could find words that would adequately describe the impact that Bob made on everybody. He exuded so much class, so much charisma. People said that we complimented each other perfectly. Bob was six feet two, his hair was so black it was almost blue; he had a very distinct widow's peak. He had large, expressive hazel eyes very much like my mother's and perfect features. He had very broad shoulders and a narrow waist. Even his hands and feet were beautiful. I was, and am, five feet seven. My hair was naturally very, very blond, and I wore it in a long pageboy. My eyes are sometimes blue and sometimes gray; it depends upon what I'm wearing. Bob could rest his chin on the top of my head. He said we were perfect for each other.

I still thought about Ray getting married. I tried very hard not to think about it, and I kept telling myself how lucky I was that Bob really did love me. I willed myself to fall in love with him all over again. I had really worked very hard trying NOT to love him when I didn't hear from him for so long.

I didn't even go home for Christmas and Mama and Daddy were expecting me. I know I disappointed them, but I just didn't want to leave Bob again, and I couldn't tell them that he was there.

The day after Christmas Bob and I were up town in this little bar he had discovered. Bars were not my favorite place to be, but I went with him, because we really didn't get a chance to be alone very much. Anyway, he said he thought we ought to go ahead and be married, that we loved each other, so why not just do it; that there was no point in waiting for other people's blessing, because we knew we'd never get that. Well, you've got to admit, that made sense, so I agreed.

I wonder now, though, would I have been so impetuous if I hadn't thought that Ray was getting married.

We went back to Mrs. Sandrock's and told her. She thought it was wonderful; in fact she was almost as excited as we were. She asked Bob if he'd gotten a ring. Neither of us had thought about that, and do you know what she did? She took her own ring off and gave it to Bob. We had already established the fact that we wore the same size. Then SHE called Mr. Norman and told him that I was not going to be there that night, and explained that we were going to South Carolina to be married. He asked to speak to me; he was very nice, but said if I possibly could would I come and at least be there for the first floor show (we were having special floor shows for the week between Christmas and New Year's.)

When I got to work that night all the people who worked there seemed to be as excited as I was. Becky had a blue garter (something borrowed, something blue) to lend me. The something old, I suppose, was Mrs. Sandrock's ring. I hadn't thought about the something new, so Becky gave me a new pair of stockings.

Bob had parked out behind the kitchen, so after I sang my songs in the floor show I put on my coat, and we told everybody "good-bye" and left through the kitchen. We had nearly made it out the door, when I heard the band start playing "Jingle Bells." I was supposed to be singing that, so I threw off my coat (on the kitchen floor) and rushed back on to the band stand and started singing. Bob was holding my coat and as soon as I finished my song we ran back through the kitchen, jumped in the car, and were on our way.

As soon as we got out of town, I made Bob stop and let me get in the back seat where I proceeded to change into a suit. We were heading for Bennettsville, SC. I hardly remember the trip, it seemed unbelievable that we were really on our way to be married, and to live happily ever after. I truly did believe that was the way it was meant to be.

When we got to Bennettsville it was very late. We found the court house. Some lights were on in the basement. We went in and told the man behind the counter we had come to be married. He told us we had to sign in and come back in twenty four hours. Well, that was really bad; I was supposed to sing the next night.

Well, we tried very hard to make the man marry us then, but he wouldn't, so I suggested we just go on to Wilmington and wait. We went to Kingsland and Howard's as soon as we got to Wilmington and woke them up. It was very early in the morning, still dark and they were not exactly thrilled to see us. Kingsland got up and cooked breakfast. I told her what we were going to do, and she told me I was crazy. You know, I think I probably was. Anyway, I swore her to secrecy, and then Bob took me over to Aunt Minnie's.

Ann and Mary Daniel were home for the holidays. Ann and Bobby were married and were living in Chicago. Bobby was going to school up there. I told them that we were gonna be married that night, but not Aunt Minnie. I knew she'd tell Mama, and somehow they'd have stopped us.

After lunch Ann and Mary Daniel and I lay down on Aunt Minnie's huge old antique bed to take a nap. I hadn't slept a wink the night before and I was exhausted. Anyway, they were telling me what to expect that night and what to do, etc. It was very exciting but I was so sleepy I went to sleep, and they let me sleep "till Bob came to get me.

We got back to Bennettsville about seven, we were about five hours too early, but the Justice of the Peace went ahead and married us anyway. The first thing I did was call Mrs. Sandrock and tell her. She said she'd call the club and tell them I wouldn't be there that night.

When we got back to Fayetteville Mrs. Sandrock was waiting for us. She said she'd fixed up a new room for us. She took us back and opened the door on a room filled with white roses. I had never seen so many in my life! On the bed she had arranged the most beautiful white gown and negligee. Mrs. Sandrock really was iike a fairy god mother.

Two days later Bob had gone downtown to run an errand for Mrs. Sandrock. Lizzy, the maid knocked on my door and told me I had a phone call, and it was Ray! He said he couldn't go through with his marriage, that they had called it off, and that he was coming to Fayetteville that weekend. He said there was something very important I had to consider by the time he got there, something that would affect the rest of my life. Well, the hardest thing I had ever had to do was to tell him that I was married. Of course, he knew all about Bob, cause I had told him about him when we first started dating. He said if I had made a mistake, it was not too late to change my mind. I told him "no," "I've done this, and now there's no way I can undo it." But you cannot imagine how much I wanted to tell him to please come back, how much I wished that Bob had not come back. You know, I've never even admitted this to myself until now.

I sat down and wrote Ray a long letter as soon as I hung up. I explained to him that I wished things were different, but that this was the way it had to be, and I told him to never call me again, to never write to me again. That I had made my bed, etc., etc. I told him too, that everything I had ever told him was true, that I did love him, but that there was nothing I could do about it now.

Doesn't fate play horrible tricks on us sometimes? I was really very much in love with Ray, and just think, if Bob had just waited five more days to come back, I would have married Ralph. But what is to be will be, I'm a firm believer in that. There is a reason for everything. I've never stopped thinking about Ray, though. Never stopped hoping that some day our paths might cross again. I wonder if he made it back from Korea. I've heard that so many young officers didn't. The first time I ever heard that name, Korea, Ray was talking about it, and this was several years before we went to war with North Korea. But trouble was already brewing over there, and Ray said, while he was still at Ft. Bragg, that Korea would probably be the next place he was sent. I do wonder what ever became of him. Captain McCormick heard from him after Bob and I were married and said that he really took it very hard. I really did love him. You just can't help wondering why things turn out the way they do sometimes.

I never forgave myself for loving Ray, though, and because of that I forgave Bob over and over again for so much, but now I really am getting ahead of my story.

Besides, if I hadn't married Bob, there would not have been Jennie, and Jennie was my everything, Jennie made up for all the disappointments. Jennie filled my life.

So, I went back to Texas with him and began a new life, a life so different from the one I had known.

We had only been in Houston two days when I received a phone call from my first cousin, Uncle Edwin's son, Edwin Burton. Uncle Edwin had passed away several years ago. I had never met any of his children. They were all older than I. They had moved to Houston when I was just a baby, and as far as I know Uncle Edwin never did come back to North Carolina except when he came to Grandpapa's funeral. Anyway, Edwin, like his father was a lawyer, and like his father he was in the oil business. Well, he called to invite me to lunch the next day.

152

(Actually it was more like a command.) He told me to bring my marriage license. I'm sure Daddy had called him. Well, it made me mad, but it made Bob furious! He told me I couldn't go. Well, I went, and I took the marriage license. I went up to his office and I was indignant! I was prepared to not like him at all, but the minute I saw him I was crazy about him. He was so good looking. Tall like Bob. He couldn't have been nicer. Took me to lunch at his club and introduced me to lots of people. Then he took me up to the Cattlemen's Club. I spent hours with him and when I got back home Bob was livid. He had followed us, and I don't think he thought Edwin was really my cousin.

After that I saw a lot of Edwin and his family. His wife had been the Beauty Queen at Rice and was beautiful. They had two children, a boy and a girl. Bob never did get over his dislike for Edwin, and he never would go with me when I went to see him or his family. I knew though, that Daddy was responsible for that first phone call from Edwin.

Bob didn't own a club in Houston. He didn't own anything. He lived with his mother. We lived with his mother. And it wasn't that she was well to do and could afford to support two strapping, strong young people. She worked, she had a responsible job, but back then women just didn't make a whole lot.

Bob's mother and father had been divorced years ago, and his father had married again. He was with Standard Oil and lived in Venezuela.

From all I've heard Bob's father's family was much like my own. They were originally from Danville, Ill. The town was named for them. Bob's grandmother, Jennie Daniel was an accomplished pianist, had played concerts with Pedareufsky and had several music studios in Houston. She had died when Bob was a teenager. She had much to do with his upbringing. I suppose that explains the class he exuded, and the manners that he displayed. Bob was very close to his "Mama Daniel."

I liked Bob's mother but was always a little 'ill at ease' around her. She was very professional, much disciplined and very smart. She worked cross word puzzles whenever she had a spare minute. She was very nice looking as well, with the most beautiful silver hair and dark eyes.

When Bob was around his mother he did not act like the sophisticated Bob I knew. She called him "Brother." because that's what his sister called him. (He just had one sister and no brothers.)

We both acted like children. Every day, if it wasn't raining, we'd go to Buffalo Bayou and fish, some nights we'd go frog gigging. On Sundays we'd go to Hermann Park and spend the day, we loved the zoo. Bob didn't even pretend to look for a job, and I was so stupid I didn't even ask how much money we had. He just seemed to always have enough.

Finally, though, I heard his mother tell him that he needed to get a job. That she couldn't continue to support us. I was MORTIFIED! I couldn't believe that Bob didn't have ANY money. Well, the next day I went downtown, and I got a job. I certainly was not going to let his mother support me. I went to work with Foley Bros., a huge department store. Bob got a job as a draftsman with some company, at least, that's what he told me. He'd go down town with me every day, and he'd get home the same time I did every afternoon.

You know what, I never, until I started writing this, realized just how dumb I really was. Why couldn't I see things the way they really were? Was I really an idiot? I wanted to see Bob the way I first saw him, I had to believe in him. I couldn't admit, even to myself, what a mess I'd made of my life. And I loved him, more and more every day. And love DOES blind us.

Finally, it became apparent that Bob didn't have a job; he said he just hadn't been able to find one. His sister Boots' husband was comptroller of a large company in Carbondale, Ill. She said we should move up there, that her husband would give him a job. So Bob went to Carbondale and I went home to stay until he worked a while and found an apartment for us.

I enjoyed being home again. I had thought, until I moved to Houston, that Wilmington was the hottest place in the world. Believe me; compared to Houston, Wilmington was not so bad. I heard from Bob often. He was working and was looking for a place for us to live. Then, out of a clear blue sky, I got a letter from him post marked "Houston." He had gone back to his mother's, and wanted me to come back to Houston right away. Well, of course, Mama and Daddy didn't want me to go, but I went.

I had only been back in Houston for a little while when Bob asked me one day, "If you could go any place in the world, where would you want to go?" I didn't even hesitate, I replied, "San Francisco." Bob said if I would wash my clothes, he'd iron them. I had never ironed anything, but he had learned how when he was in the Marines.

The very next day we left on a Greyhound bus. I had never flown, and I was very much afraid to fly. We stopped in Dallas for two nights; there was a club there that Bob liked. Then we stopped in Los Angeles for one night. We could have flown cheaper.

156

Sweetheart of the Carolinas

We got to San Francisco late one afternoon, with no idea in the world where we were going to stay or anything. I suggested a residence hotel; there are lots of them out there. So that's what we did. The St. Anna, on the corner of Geary and Jones is the one we chose. Our room was on the top floor over looking Geary St. We stayed there for almost a year; apartments were almost impossible to find.

San Francisco again

San Francisco ♫

Being in San Francisco then was like being in wonderland; there was something magical about that city. Everyday was an adventure, we took in everything, and there was so much to see. When I look back now it hardly seems real. We were so happy just to be together and to be together in this wonderful place, on our own with our whole lives in front of us. And the world looked so bright then, nothing seemed impossible. I really thought it would always be this way. We were alone together in a world of our own. We didn't know a living soul within thousands of miles but each other. That didn't last very long, for everywhere we went, everybody we saw seemed to embrace us, to welcome us.

After a while, though, our money ran out. I kept asking him, "Shouldn't we be looking for jobs?" but he said "No, we'll do that later." Then one day, with no warning at all, he just casually mentioned that he'd better start looking for something to do, that we were getting low on money. I asked him how low, and he said, "Well, we have enough for next weeks rent but not much more."

I just about had a fit then. I could not believe it! We'd been spending money like water. We went to all the best restaurants, all the best clubs, and now to find out that we were almost penniless. How in the world would we even be able to eat next week if he just had enough for the hotel bill?

The next day I answered an ad in the paper for a hat check girl at the St. Francis Hotel. I knew with a job like that I'd get tips, at least that way we could eat. They hired me, but told me to come to work that night wearing a smart looking black dress. Well, I had left most of my clothes in Houston. This was 1947, the year that the "new look" came in. Almost overnight hemlines dropped 12 inches, so I had left lots of good looking black dresses and eight beautiful suits in Houston, because I thought I'd just get new clothes in San Francisco.

I had bought a pretty suit, but it wasn't black so I couldn't take that job, and I certainly couldn't afford to buy anything then.

I answered another ad; this one was for an usherette. (I figured if Lauren Bacall could do it, I could, too.) They furnished a uniform, so I took the job. It was in a very old, very beautiful, really elegant theater. The whole time I was there "Black Narcissus" with Deborah Kerr was playing. The uniform

160

they gave me to wear was really good looking, a beautiful shade of green with gold epaulets on the shoulders.

Bob came in one day (He could get in free, because I worked there.) He told me to come get him at three o'clock that he had an appointment with the Schick Shaver Co. at 3:30, and he was afraid he might go to sleep. He'd been everywhere looking for a job, and he was so tired.

Well, at 3 o'clock I did have to wake him up. He told me to wish him luck and he left.

At five o'clock he came back and told me to quit my job. In fact, he went to the manager and told him I had to leave. (He'd gotten the job.)

That night we had steak for supper. We'd been practically living on baloney sandwiches for a week. But you know, even that wasn't so bad. Everything seemed like an adventure then.

We became acquainted with this really nice older man who lived in a hotel across the street from ours, a Mr. Robinson. He had been a professor at Harvard for several years, but was an artist and was on sabbatical to paint. He really took us under his wing. Mr. Robinson and his friend, a very nice, interesting lady, introduced us to wonderful restaurants that were not tourist traps. "Robinski," as Bob called him, was originally from San Francisco, so he knew all the best places to eat. He was certainly one of the most memorable people I have ever known, and he had the most wonderful sense of humor. He said you didn't have to be around Bob or me 10 minutes to know that we had been educated in the finest schools. He was wrong, of course. Whatever we had was born in us.

I was ready to start singing again. At first Bob said no, but I knew I could make more money doing that than anything else, and really, I didn't know how to do anything else.

The Savoy Club was no more, neither was Diamond Lil's. Macy's Department Store now occupied their space. So I went back to see the same agent that I saw before, remember? The first time I was in San Francisco? This time he sent me to a place called "The Irisher." That was a fun place to be, too. Pat Kelly was the owner, and he was the nicest man in the world. Instead of mustaches (like Diamond Lil's) on the tables, there were shamrocks. Everything was green, everything was Irish, except me, but I loved it there.

This woman I had known at the Savoy Club, Jackie Sherman, was working there. She had played in the cocktail lounge at the Savoy Club, and here she alternated with the band. It was good to see somebody I remembered.

Bob would come down to meet me every night. I told him that was silly, because he had to get up early and go to work, but he still came every night. When he got home from work we'd go to supper, then he'd walk me to work. Sometimes on the way home at night we'd stop somewhere and eat again. (I was always hungry.) Sometimes (but not often) I'd get up and go to breakfast with him.

I sang at the "Irisher" for six weeks, and then I sang at a club just around the corner, "The Players Club" for a month. After that I sang at "Raphael's Frolic Room" for a month, and then I went back to the "Irisher."

On Saturdays I'd go with Bob to a western movie, and then he'd go with me to one of "my" movies. If I didn't have to work that night we'd sometimes go to the Marines Memorial, then we'd have dinner at one of the fine restaurants we knew. My favorite was Bon Gusto out at North Beach.

On Sundays we'd often go out to Fisherman's Wharf and spend the day. We'd walk around and look at the boats and have lunch at one of the fine restaurants out there. Sometimes

Bob would fish (He loved to fish) on the pier across from Alcatraz.

Several times when we were walking around Fisherman's Wharf, we noticed an elderly woman walking around by herself. Bob said he bet that when she was young, she and her husband used to come out there like we were doing and walk around; that more than likely her husband was dead and that she came out there now, because she, somehow, felt closer to him.

I think about that a lot, and if I ever go back to San Francisco, you better believe I'll probably spend at least one Sunday at Fisherman's Wharf. Wouldn't it be wonderful if we could just go back to where we used to be and live life all over again? I'd be so much smarter if I had a second chance. "Backward, turn backward oh time in your flight", remember that? It keeps running through my mind. I've been able to take, or rather to STAND a lot in this last part of my life, just because I'm so thankful for the first part of my life. Does that make sense? Like the song "When I Grow Too Old to Dream, I'll Have You to Remember." I love that song.

We loved Golden Gate Park. I especially liked the tea room. We enjoyed the band concerts, and the Japanese Tea

164

Room. We spent many hours at Flash Ackers Zoo. We both liked animals, Bob even more than I.

Everything was so new then, so wonderful. Nothing seemed impossible. As long as we had each other nothing else mattered.

I look back now, and it's hard to believe that I could ever have been so credulous, so naive. It never entered my head that it wouldn't always be like this, or that Bob could ever love any body but me. I knew I'd always love him. Maybe, I just still believed in fairy tales. If we live long enough we all have to grow up, to face facts, to look reality in the face. For some of us that reality is hard to face. For me it was almost impossible. I'm really getting ahead of my story now.

Bob started getting sick a lot. One day he even had to come home from work. I was terribly worried about him, (Back then the only thing I worried about was that one of us, or anybody that I loved, might get sick) then I found out that I was pregnant. I couldn't believe it. Oh, I was so happy to think that now we were going to have a baby of our own. Nothing ever made me as proud as that. Sometimes I'd wake up at night and worry that I might be too happy, that something bad was bound to happen.

Bob bought me a new Bulova watch, one with diamonds. He said every time I looked at it, it would remind me to be careful, that now I was going to be a Mother, and I had to really take care of myself. I didn't get sick at all, in fact I felt wonderful.

After we found out we were going to have a baby we decided that we really did need to get an apartment. Nearly everyday, while Bob was at work, I'd go around answering ads for an apartment to rent. You know, it was almost impossible. There were just not that many for rent, and when I'd get to wherever the apartment was located, there'd always be about twenty people ahead of me. If you were lucky enough to be the first one there, you had to give the renter a big bonus. (I never was the first.) It was awfully discouraging.

This man, Freddy, (I can't remember his last name) was a regular customer at the Irisher. He usually came in early, before the crowd came in. Most of the time he just came in to have a cup of coffee. Pat Kelly was a friend of his. If people hadn't come in yet, I'd usually sit down and have coffee with him. He knew everybody who worked there so sometimes we'd have a table full. Anyway, I'd always talk about looking for an apartment and how hopeless it seemed. I felt perfectly at home with all those people. Of course, their back grounds couldn't have been more different from mine. These people were very sophisticated, they'd been everywhere and they knew so many really big celebrities. For instance, Bing Crosby always came in the club when he was in town. (He never came while I was there, and I was always disappointed.) But they knew so many really big stars. I was completely fascinated by them and they seemed to be with me. They called me 'you all, Carolina' I didn't mind. I knew they were my friends.

Anyway, one night as soon as I sat down Freddy said. "Don't tell me, you're worn out because you've been looking for apartments all day," and I said, "Well, I have, and there just aren't any." Then he said, "I'll tell you the truth, I'm tired of hearing you talk about it, in fact, I'm so sick of it, I don't want to ever hear you talk about it again."

I couldn't believe he was talking like this. He'd always been so nice to me. I started to get up from the table, and he said, "Sit down, I'm not through yet."

Well, I really thought he'd lost his mind. I looked at Jackie Sherman, and she wouldn't even look at me. I was almost about to cry. Nobody had ever been so rude to me before.

Then he said, "I'm so tired of hearing you gripe, that I went out today and bought an apartment house, just so you and that husband of yours and that little baby that is coming will have a place to live." Then he started laughing, and everybody at the table was laughing. They were all in cahoots with him, and they really thought they'd pulled a fast one on me. They had.

So that's how we finally found an apartment. We were just thrilled to death. Bob and I moved in the following Sunday, sight unseen. We were so delighted to have our own place. We were crazy about our apartment. It was way out close to Twin Peaks. We had the first floor flat and Freddy's parents lived just above us. There was a young couple not much older than we were on the third floor.

Right away, I started (trying) to learn to cook. Rose, Freddy's mother, taught me a lot. So did the girl on the third floor, she was Italian and I learned a lot about cooking from her.

There were three girls in Bob's office that I had gotten to know well, and there was a man that became Bob's good friend. Often, if I didn't have to work, they'd all come over to our apartment for supper. I was probably a terrible cook, but they seemed to enjoy it.

168

Everybody at Bob's office seemed to be crazy about him. He was really doing so well, and I couldn't have been happier.

I'm terribly superstitious. I wouldn't buy any clothes for the baby, because I was so afraid something might happen. Freddie's mother, though, was almost as excited as we were, and every time she went downtown she'd buy something beautiful for the baby.

You know, people really have been nice to me, haven't they? I've been blessed in many ways.

I still hadn't been to the doctor. Three times Bob got off work early to go with me, and then we'd decide not to go. I felt so good, and I ate very nourishing food. Every day for lunch I'd have calves liver and bacon with onions, and I drank, at least, a quart of milk a day. When I finally did go to the doctor, he said what ever I had been doing was right, because he had never seen anybody in better shape than I was. He x-rayed me, though, because I have very small bones to be as tall as I am, but I was fine.

By this time I was about five months along, but I wasn't showing yet, and I had planned to keep on singing for, at least, a month or two longer. In fact, Bob and I had talked it over and decided that for the next two months we would save every penny I made for the hospital bill. (We didn't have hospitalization.)

Then, as I've said before, there's always a 'then'.

Bob called about 2 o'clock one afternoon, and told me to get dressed and come to his office, to get there as quickly as I could. When I got to his office he was waiting. He took me into his boss, Mr. Gilroy's office, and introduced me to a man from the home office in Stanford, Conn. This man wanted to interview me. He asked me how I would feel about moving back to Houston. I didn't really like Houston that much, but I didn't tell him that. Anyway, the gist of the whole thing was that they were so pleased with Bob's performance that they wanted to make him manager of a branch they were opening in Houston.

Well, this was like a dream come true, and so fast. (See, Bob was proving them all wrong!) I was so proud of him. (We were both so proud of him.) The promotion came through, along with a large check for expenses. Bob insisted that I quit my job immediately. They couldn't do enough for us. Everybody took us out, or had us to dinner.

We bought new clothes, we took our friends out. We were like the Jefferson's, moving on up. Everything was coming up roses! Life was good.

We had spent most of the expense money, but still had enough for the plane fare. Bob said we had to fly back to Houston that we couldn't risk going any other way.

It was almost time for us to leave. Bob left for work early so he could go by and pick up our plane tickets. He told me to start getting everything together. We didn't have a lot to pack, just our clothes, really, and a few things that we'd collected. Later that morning I went upstairs and had coffee with Rose, Freddie's mother. She was so sorry we were leaving; she'd been looking forward to the baby. I would miss her; she had been so nice to me. Rose's phone rang, and it was Bob, He'd been trying to reach me downstairs and wondered if I was there. When I answered the phone he sounded very "down". He told me to go back to our apartment and call him. It sounded rather ominous.

When I called him he told me that everything had been called off, that we wouldn't be going back to Houston, so not to worry about packing. He wouldn't explain, just said we'd talk when he got home.

What had happened was this: At the last minute they had checked his references and they had found out that, one, he was only 24, not 27 as he had told them, and, two, they checked with his brother-in-law, Smitty, and he had told them that he had only worked for him a few weeks, not three years, as he had told them he had. They still wanted him to work for the company, thought he had a lot of potential but that he needed much more experience than he had.

I had quit my job, you know, and I was ashamed to ask for it back, because I was beginning to show. Bob had to pay back that big expense money, (that we had spent.) He worked every day, though, and finally paid every cent back. That took quite a while, and we had to live just on his salary.

By the time he got through paying that money back I was over eight months along. We didn't have any money saved for the hospital bill, and I hadn't even been to the doctor. I was not all that worried, though, I just knew somehow we'd make it, and I was so relieved when that money was all paid back. Bob, on the other hand, was very "down," very despondent.

And then, just two days after he had paid all that money back, it began; the beginning of the end. My world would never again be the same.

I was so happy; we had finally finished paying Bob's company back. Bob, though, seemed to have something on his mind. I knew he was worrying about the hospital bill. I, though, didn't even care about going to the hospital. I'd just have the baby at home if necessary. (I had no idea what it was like.) It's hard to believe that anybody could be as stupid as I was. Maybe I was protected too much from the real world. I don't know; maybe I was just dumb.

Anyway, that Sunday, I was in the kitchen getting ready to fix lunch. Bob came in and said he was going to this little bar around the corner (San Francisco has a million bars) to get cigarettes, and would be right back. When he didn't come back right away, I wasn't even worried, I just figured he had seen somebody he knew and had decided to have a drink with them.

I finished fixing lunch and waited. Then I began to get mad, what on earth could be keeping him? I didn't even know the name of that bar, so I couldn't call. Finally, I just went around there. The bartender hadn't seen him. By this time I was beginning to get panicky. I just couldn't understand it.

Hours passed and it was getting dark and still no sign of him. Rose came down to bring us some cake she had made. She could tell something was wrong, I didn't know what to do, so I told her.

Well, she just insisted that I go upstairs and spend the night with her, but I wouldn't. I had never spent a night by myself before. I wasn't afraid, but I couldn't sleep in our bed. I lay down on the sofa in the living room, but I couldn't go to sleep. That was one of the longest nights of my life.

The next morning about 10 o'clock Mr. Gilroy, Bob's boss came over. He wanted to see Bob, and I told him the truth. I was almost sick, I was so worried. I was afraid something terrible had happened to him. Mr. Gilroy told me not to worry. He said he had to go back to his office, but asked that I let him know as soon as I heard something.

About an hour later one of the girls in Bob's office, Lois, just appeared at my door. She said Mr. Gilroy had given her the day off so she could spend it with me. I was really almost crazy I was so worried. I hadn't eaten anything since Bob had been gone; she reminded me about the baby and practically MADE me go with her to a tea room nearby. I just could not eat.

I kept the radio on constantly. That afternoon about 5 o'clock a bulletin came on that an unidentified man had jumped off the Golden Gate Bridge. Well, then I really did go all to pieces. Rose and Lois both tried to tell me that San Francisco was a big city and that in all probability it was not him, but I was just crazy with fear.

A little after 6 o'clock Mr. and Mrs. Gilroy came over. They wanted me to go home with them and spend the night. I wouldn't do it. I just simply could not leave until I heard something. Mr. Gilroy then asked me for Daddy's name and phone number, and I really went all to pieces. I KNEW something horrible must have happened to Bob. I was inconsolable.

Finally, Mr. Gilroy told me (I am sure he didn't want to tell me, but I think he just didn't know what else to do) that yesterday, Sunday, Bob had gone to the his office building, had signed in and had gone up to his office and opened the safe. He had taken the exact amount of money that he had paid back, his expense account money, and apparently vanished. He said he didn't think, for a minute, that the jumper was Bob, that they hadn't recovered the man's body, so he couldn't be positive, but that Bob had just probably taken off for parts unknown.

Another thing he told me was that he, Mr. Gilroy, had been promoted and was moving to Stanford, Conn., and that they were going to offer Bob his job as manager of the San Francisco office next month. They had planned to tell him next week.

Oh, how I wish they had told him.

I would not go home with them, and I wouldn't go upstairs and spend the night with Rose, either. I still couldn't sleep in our bed, so I put sheets and a pillow on the sofa again. I was so tired and hoped I'd be able to sleep that night. I was kneeling down, saying my prayers when I heard something in the kitchen. I ran into the kitchen and heard a soft tapping at the door. I didn't even think to be frightened, just ran to the door and opened it and there stood Bob. Well, then I almost collapsed. What a blessed relief, oh, thank goodness, it was him!

He started crying, crying like a baby, I had never heard him cry before. He just held me and kept saying how sorry he was. And you know I wasn't even mad. I just felt so awfully sorry for him. I loved him with my whole heart and soul, but somehow I knew that our lives had been changed forever, that we'd never again get back what we had.

Bob thought the police were looking for him, he was really afraid. He told me to pack a bag, that we were going uptown and spend the night in a hotel. I told him he had to call Mr. Gilroy because I had promised him that I would call him as soon as I had heard anything. He said "no." He said we both needed a good night's sleep and that tomorrow morning I could call Mr. Gilroy.

So that's what we did. We went uptown and registered at a hotel. He even used an assumed name.

The next morning, early, I called Mr. Gilroy at home. He, of course, wanted to talk to Bob. Bob had already told me to tell him that he would meet him out at Fisherman's Wharf in a little restaurant that we knew. Mr. Gilroy, gentleman that he was, agreed to do that. (He could have demanded that Bob speak to him then.)

So Bob left to meet him, and I stayed at the hotel to wait. After what seemed like a very long time Bob came back. He said that Mr. Gilroy said that he would not press charges, but that the money must be paid back immediately, and of course Bob could no longer work for the company. Bob said there were tears in Mr. Gilroy's eyes when he told him that. It's terrible to lose faith in people, especially people you care about.

He told him too, that he must come to the office and pay the money back in front of his co-workers.

Bob had spent the money. I never did find out what he did with it. I tried, very hard, not to imagine what he did with it. It was all like a nightmare.

He borrowed the money from Freddy's best friend, who had become our friend, too. (A very good friend.) He then went up to see Mr. Gilroy, and I know that was a very hard thing to do, a very humiliating thing to do, and he gave Mr. Gilroy all the money. He told me that everybody seemed sad. I can only imagine what it must have been like. You see, they all really liked him. Even the ones who had been with the company much longer than he, had never shown any resentment when he was promoted. And they liked me too, and I liked them. I have often thought about them. He came back to the hotel to get me and we went back to our apartment.

Well, Freddy was furious with Bob, first for worrying me, and second for borrowing money from his friend. He told Bob he had to move. He told me I could stay, in fact, Rose, his mother, insisted that I stay with her. I don't have to tell you I wouldn't do that.

So Bob and I moved into yet another residence hotel. We, of course, had very little money. I couldn't look for a job, I was really showing. Bob got a job as a waiter in a very good restaurant. He had never done that kind of work before and apparently it was very hard, because he would look so tired when he came home. He was ashamed to even look for a good job, because he couldn't give Schick as a reference. Oh, it was awful! We were just at our wits end. I was eight and a half months pregnant, and I was so hungry all the time. When I'd go in the restaurant next to our hotel to eat, I would order the cheapest thing on the menu. I craved water melon, but I couldn't afford the extra 25 cents that a slice of water melon cost then. Somebody in the restaurant was always eating some. It's totally unbelievable how quickly your life can change.

I didn't tell Mama and Daddy anything. I knew they'd make me come home, besides I didn't want to worry then.

Finally though, Bob called his mother, and she sent us the money to go back to Texas. I can only imagine how she must have felt. She had been so proud of Bob for really buckling down and working so hard.

I've often wondered, too. If only they hadn't built our hopes up and given us that money, if only we could have done what we had planned, and I could have worked a little longer and saved the money for the hospital bill, would we have stayed in San Francisco? I think we probably would have. We were doing so well, and we were so happy. I could have kept on singing and making good money.

So, we went back to Texas on another Greyhound Bus. That's a long, long way, believe me, especially when you're nearly nine months pregnant, and this time we didn't stop any where and sleep.

Bob's Mother couldn't believe I hadn't seen a doctor. She was absolutely overcome with shock. The next day, after we got there, I was sitting in a doctor's office. Well, the doctor couldn't believe it either, and he REALLY couldn't believe that we had ridden a bus all the way from San Francisco. He said Bob and I were the bravest two people he could imagine. (He didn't say CRAZY, but I think that's what he thought.)

Anyway, after a thorough examination, he found me to be in tip top shape. I hadn't been concerned about that at all. Mama was sort of a health nut. Even before it was fashionable, she made me take plenty of exercise, and even more important, she had instilled in me the fact that good nutrition was most important, and I was very particular about what I ate.

180

Bob wouldn't even look for a good job, because he was afraid they'd find out about Schick, so he went to work for a friend of his who had just started a delivery business.

He would come home two or three times a day just to check on me. He was so worried about me going to the hospital. I tried to tell him not to worry; I wasn't afraid at all, besides I've always been a lot stronger than I looked. Every night after supper we'd go for a long walk, a long walk. His mother told him I needed exercise.

We had been back in Texas about a month, and I was two weeks overdue. I just wanted to hurry up and have this baby. (You do get so tired of waiting.) Anyway, Bob and his mother and I were playing bridge one night after we had come back from our walk when I began having pains. Bob got me to the hospital post haste. The doctor came and told Bob to go home; he said it would be, at least, sometime tomorrow. He wanted to keep me in the hospital, but told him to go home and come back the next day. In those days the father was not allowed in the delivery room.

Almost as soon as he left the pains got worse. I had told the doctor I did not want that spinal that he said he was going to give me, and he said he wouldn't give it to me unless I asked. Well, believe me, I asked.

Jennie came into this world at 9:30 the next morning. I had been screaming and groaning and carrying on something awful, but when it was over and the doctor laid her on my stomach and I saw that little face, so indignant and so mad, I started laughing and everybody in the delivery room was laughing. I had never been so proud of anything in my life.

From that moment on my life would change forever. The sheer wonder of it almost overwhelmed me. This little baby, part of me and part of Bob, became the single most important person in my life. Everything and everybody, including me, became second to her. She was the best part of me. She was my life. Having her was the best thing that ever happened to me.

We named her Jennie, after her great grandmother, Jennie Daniel. I was so glad Bob's grandmother was named Jennie, because in our family it was an unwritten law, you could only have family names. Her full name was Jennifer Karline (Karline after Bob's father Karl) Daniel. Later on she became Jennifer Kingsland Daniel, Mama couldn't stand made up names. To me, she was always just Jennie.

I always get ahead of myself, don't I?

Life after Bob ♫

That was a very long time ago, so much has happened since then, not a lot very good. Still, I shouldn't say that, I loved having a little girl; I wouldn't trade having her for anything. Nothing has ever seemed so natural, so real, as having my own little girl, and never have I ever been so proud of anything. I loved her completely, with all my heart. I wonder sometimes, did I love her too much? Is it possible to do that? I never took her for granted. I thanked God for her every day, several times every day. I was so afraid something would happen to her. But I can't say I was happy, because I never got over Bob. I wonder what it would have been like if we'd stayed together as a family. If only he hadn't taken that money and if his promotion had come through and we had stayed in San Francisco. Sometimes I try to imagine how it might have been. How different our lives could have been, should have been. But it didn't happen that way, and it just broke my heart, I was so sure that Bob and I would always be together, that God made me for him and him for me, that was the way it was meant to be. I'm getting ahead of my story again.

We lived with his mother, and I don't suppose that is ever easy for anybody, especially when money is an item. At first it wasn't so bad, but then Bob started drinking again, and he lost his job. I am sure his mother was worried to death. She and I began to not like each other very much. Now I can see her side, I couldn't then. She told me that Bob loved me more than she ever could imagine him loving anybody and that I should stand up and demand that he buckle down and get a good job. I never had demanded anything of anybody in my whole life; I had never had to do that. Everything just seemed to work out right, up until then anyway. Bob even told me that if we continued to live with his Mother we wouldn't be together a year from then, just like I could do something about it. I was still such a child. I just kept hoping things would work out, and I really believed they would. It never dawned on me to move and get a job. Jennie took up all my time, I never got enough sleep, I even lost my appetite, and I just kept getting thinner. I'm sure I looked anorexic. I looked so bad and felt so bad that I knew there was no point in even trying to sing. Back then the way you looked was just as important as how you sounded.

Deep down inside, though I wouldn't admit it even to my self, I knew it wasn't going to last. I remember rocking Jennie and singing "What'll I Do." That song kept running through my mind. You see there has always been another me, a smarter me. But the predominant me was the believer, the one who wouldn't face facts. I wanted so much for it to last. The hardest thing to admit is defeat. And so I hid from reality. I couldn't, I wouldn't believe that loving Bob was a lost cause, that there was no future for Bob and me.

Mama and Daddy kept trying to get Jennie and me to go back to North Carolina, so that's what we did. Bob didn't want us to, but the fact is, he got there before we did.

Mama and Daddy were not at all happy to see him. Daddy got an apartment for us, though, and Bob started looking for a job. Everyday Daddy would come over and complain to me about Bob, he wouldn't say anything to him about it, just to me. Then I would complain to Bob when he got home. I was almost crazy, I even told him to leave. I told you what a good 'fusser' Mama was. Well, I was almost as good. I just couldn't understand. Really, I suppose, I almost lost my mind.

Then one night Bob didn't come home. Two days later he called collect, but Daddy answered the phone and wouldn't let me accept the call. Bob had gone back to Texas, but he wrote often. He said how much he missed us and talked about looking for a job and a place for us. But then the letters stopped coming and I just had too much pride to beg him to come and get us; and I wouldn't even ask him for money for Jennie. My heart was just broken, and I thought it was my fault because I was so thin and looked so bad. All my self confidence had vanished. I hated myself for looking so bad. I thought that was why he left. It all seems like a bad dream now, it did then too. I blamed myself; it was my fault for looking so bad. Bob hated ugly people. Really, I was almost crazy.

Jennie was walking by now, and she was the cutest, the smartest little girl. I used to marvel at the things she did. Everything I tried to teach her, she learned so fast. And she was so pretty, had these huge blue, expressive eyes and golden red ringlets. I used to brush and brush her hair after her bath, and it was so sad, there was no one but me to see it. Oh, how I longed for Bob to see her.

Sometimes after I'd go to bed at night, I'd imagine that Bob was across the street watching, but that he was afraid to come in, because of Daddy. I missed him so much. I just couldn't believe it. I wanted to call him, to write to him, to just go back to Texas and see him, but I didn't, I wouldn't, I couldn't.

Mama and Daddy made me go to the doctor immediately, and I started taking liver shots and Vitamin B12 shots and all kinds of vitamins. Gradually my appetite came back, I bought new clothes. I was planning to go back to work.

Foy, remember her, invited Jennie and me to spend the summer with her family at their beach house. Mama and Daddy thought that was a wonderful idea. I know they were worried about me and I suppose they thought a summer at the beach would somehow get 'me' back, because I certainly was not the real me then.

I enjoyed that summer as much as I could have enjoyed anything, and I know the fresh air and sunshine were good for Jennie and for me, but I tell you I was mighty sad. I had been so sure that Bob loved us as much as I loved him. I thought that if you wanted something bad enough, you somehow got it. Again, just like before we were married, I had to work very hard to make myself stop loving him. It didn't work though. Maybe I was really just born to sing the blues. I don't mean the sort of blues, or what they call the blues now. I mean the minor keys; that beat like nothing else, the aloneness and the despair. That's how it was. My world was in a minor key.

Anyway, at the end of summer Foy insisted that I go back to Charlotte with them and get a job and live with them 'til I got on my feet.

Up until then Jennie had been with me around the clock. She was the cutest little girl, but she really had a mind of her own. She refused to eat a bite unless I was with her. I had to work, but she was not happy with me working. Every day the colored girl who looked after Foy's little boy and Jennie would call me at lunch time, and I'd have to go home to feed her. Finally Mama and Daddy decided to keep her. She loved them and they loved her. I would go home every weekend.

She used to come with Daddy to the bus station to meet me every week; I can still see that happy little face, so glad to see her "Mama Bill." I can still see that sad little face, when I'd be leaving to go back to Charlotte. Nobody knows how I wish I could go back to then and somehow make her happier. There are so many things I'd do differently if I could. I was luckier than I realized, I had the most important thing in the world, I had her.

I wish I had realized this then, I'd have done what I couldn't do then. I'd have, somehow, gotten the strength to let Bob go from my heart and my mind. Still I wonder if you can ever, really, do that. When someone fills your life so completely, can you ever really ever let go? He filled such a big part of my life, that when he left there was nothing that could ever fill the void that he left. We learn to live with the emptiness, but it is so hard. If I hadn't had Jennie I don't honestly know if I could have made it. We don't get second chances at life either, we have to live with our mistakes and go

188

on. "When You're Alone on the Street of Regret," That was a song I used to sing. I've lived on that street for a long time now. Now, though, I have learned that you can't stay on that street. We have regrets, sure, but there is not one thing we can do about them. We have to grit our teeth and take what comes, take it and move on.

Things have a way of working out though; sometimes for the good, sometimes for the bad. Carolyn and Walter were married and living in Charlotte still. Carolyn was very concerned about me, everybody was. Everybody but Clarence. He never forgave me for marrying Bob. He was nice enough, but just not like he used to be. I think he was just so disappointed in me.

Carolyn called me one day at work, and told me that Jimmy Jett was in town. (Remember, from the Plantation?) His sister lived in Charlotte and he had come to visit her. When he found out I was in Charlotte he called and invited me out to dinner. He said I had to start back singing again, that that would be the best therapy for me. He introduced me to Billy Knoff, a classmate of his in Chapel Hill years ago. They had both worked with the Les Brown Orchestra. Jimmy made me sing for Billy, and he liked me. He had a really good orchestra, the best in Charlotte, but he also had a vocalist with whom he was very well pleased. He said he'd do what he could though.

One night soon after that he called and told me that the singer at the Flamingo Club was unable to sing that night and for me to immediately go down there, that this was a wonderful opportunity. I had just washed my hair and was ready for bed, but I got dressed and called a taxi and went to the Flamingo. I was kind of nervous, because I hadn't sung since before Jennie was born.

The Flamingo was a beautiful club, the acoustics were wonderful. There was a small combo from New York. I gave the piano player my key, told him what I wanted to sing and got up on the band stand and sang and got the job. And just like that I was on the road back to being me.

I was delighted to find that the Food and Beverage Director at the Ocean Forest Hotel in Myrtle Beach was acting manager of the Flamingo. (He and the owner of the club were partners, and the manager was away on his honeymoon.)

I stayed at the Flamingo several months and really enjoyed it. Every night after work I'd go with the musicians to the White Front Grill to eat. (It was the only place in Charlotte open that late.) I still had my day job too, so I didn't get much sleep, but I started gaining weight. I was so glad. Of course I couldn't go to see Jennie on weekends, and I didn't like that. I got up my nerve though and finally flew just so I could spend a few hours with her. Finally Mama and Daddy moved to Charlotte so I could be with Jennie more.

I think about them now, about how good they were to Jennie and to me, and I know how worried they were about me. Then, though, I was mad with Daddy. I blamed him for Bob leaving. I could blame everybody, even me, but not Bob.

After the Flamingo I didn't have any trouble at all finding places to sing. In fact, I got calls from large hotels, the Henry Grady in Atlanta and a large hotel in Winston Salem and several others. Back then all the better hotels had orchestras. I don't know how they found out about me. I stayed in Charlotte though and worked with local bands.

Daddy got a letter from his sister saying she had heard from their nephew in Houston. (Edwin, remember?) I had seen a lot of him and his family when I lived there. She sent the letter to Daddy.

That letter almost did me in.

It said that Bob had married again and had a baby. How could he be married to somebody else? WE were married! I couldn't believe it. There are no words to describe how that made me feel, but I'll tell you this, it broke my heart all over again.

You see, I had never stopped hoping that he would just appear one day and life would be 'right' again. It almost killed me to have to accept the fact that he loved somebody else. I didn't think he could. The thought that Bob could love somebody else was unbelievable, it was unimaginable.

I got through it, though. It took all the strength I could muster, but I took it. Sometimes there is nothing else we CAN do. We have to take it. I've taken a lot since then. That was just one of the first. I thought then that nothing could ever hurt so much. I found out different though, and I had to take that, too.

I was still quite young then, but I was totally disillusioned. I had no interest, at all, in meeting another man. My 'prince charming' had come, and he was gone. There couldn't be anybody else for me.

I must have thought I looked worse than I did. People still gathered around the band stand when I stood up to sing, but it never was the same. I was totally disillusioned, shattered.

Jennie filled my life; she was my reason for being in this world. I had lost everything, everything but her, and I fiercely held on to her. As long as I had her nothing else really mattered.

I know now I should have looked for a father for Jennie, somebody to watch over both of us, but being practical and sensible were never my long suit. The ones I liked were always the wrong ones. The "right" ones, the ones who really liked me, I usually couldn't stand. To tell you the truth there never was, really, a right one for me, they were all just imitations, bad imitations at that. Maybe if, somehow, Ray had come back, remember the one in Fayetteville? He was the real thing. I never heard from him again though.

I wonder sometimes how different my life might have been if Bob had just waited a week to show up in Fayetteville, and I had married Ray. I wouldn't have had Jennie though, and she made up for everything. So I never could even really wish for that.

Daddy's business took him to Richmond when Jennie was four years old, and I moved with them. I never wanted to be separated from Jennie again.

We Moved to Richmond

Jennie's Side

The way I think she would have told it.

I had just turned four when we moved to Richmond, my Mama Bill and Mammy and Da and me. Actually I had just turned four the day before we moved and Bill, that's what I called my Mama, had bought me the biggest tricycle I had ever seen. My Da fussed with Bill 'cause he said she was so impractical, and why in the world hadn't she waited 'til we got to Richmond to buy that great big thing. Da fussed with Bill a lot, mainly because she let me sit up too late at night. He said little children needed to go to bed early, but I liked to sit up late after Mammy and Da went to bed, 'cause then Bill and I could discuss the day's happenings, besides most of the time she'd make pop corn. Bill said I was her very best friend, and I was. We did everything together except, of course, when she was working. Then I'd stay home with Mammy and help her cook. I loved my Mammy and Da very much. Guess you've figured out they were Bill's parents. Bill loved them too, but she said they just didn't seem to realize that she was a grown woman. They treated her pretty much the way they treated me. Bill said they bossed her too much. Anyway, that very first night we got to

Richmond, Da took us down town to watch the Christmas Parade. Bill didn't want to go really, she was just too tired she said, and Mammy felt the same way. But Da just MADE them go; he said that I shouldn't have to miss the Christmas parade. To tell you the truth it was the coldest night I had ever felt, and that was the longest parade I've ever seen. Bill unbuttoned her coat and buttoned it around me and then I was pretty warm. I was kind of glad though, to get back to our new house and go to bed, 'cause I was tired too.

I slept with Bill every night. I loved to snuggle up to her and listen to the stories she told me. Bill could tell the best stories you've ever heard. I had just turned four, like I said, so there was a whole lot I didn't know yet, but one thing I knew for sure was that Bill, my momma, loved me. Mammy and Da did too, I knew that. I loved them a lot, but I worshiped Bill. We used to sing "Side by Side" together. I knew all the words, and when we'd be riding in the back seat together going some where with Mammy and Da, we'd sing "Sonny Boy" like Al Jolson, only we'd say "Jennie Girl."

I didn't know much about my Daddy at all, only that he was the handsomest man in the whole world. That's what Bill told me and that I was a lot like him. Mammy and Da didn't care very much for him, I could tell that. To tell you the truth I didn't miss him very much 'cause I couldn't remember him at all. I think Bill missed him though, but she said that I made up for everything, and that as long as she had me she really didn't need anything else. Like I said before we were always side by side, we had each other, and that's what mattered.

Bill got a job at Thalheimer's the very next day after we moved to Richmond. It was in the Cosmetic Department and she really liked it there. She was in the Yardley Department and every night when she came home she smelled like lavender. Bill loved perfume. I did too. She said she wished she could keep that job 'cause she really did enjoy it, but she knew she couldn't. It just didn't pay enough, so on her day off she'd go to the employment office. Somebody told her that the best paying jobs in town were at the FFV cookie company so she told them she'd like to work there. The people at the employment office told her that no way would they send her there. In the first place it was really hard work, besides she just wasn't the type to work in a cookie factory. So then she went to Reynolds Metals Co. and got a job there in the office and she hated office work. Besides that she couldn't stand her supervisor. She was mean as the devil, that's what Bill said, and besides that she thought Bill was spoiled. She also said that people in North Carolina were lazy 'cause they took naps in the afternoon. Anyway, Bill kept going to the employment office and finally she got a job that was not quite as boring as office work. Virginia Stage Lines was opening a beautiful new bus terminal and she got a job there in Tours and Information. Right off the bat she practically memorized the Russell's Guide and all she had to do was talk to people on the phone and tell them where to go. It got to be very aggravating, especially when a holiday was coming up, but like she said, every time she hung up the phone she was through 'til the next time it rang. Sometimes four or five of them rang at the same time, but somehow she kept up with it. Back then nice people rode the bus, and the people who worked there were nice, too.

The only thing she really liked to do, of course, was sing. There was a really good combo on one of the Television Stations, so she went to the studio and met them. Their show was being canceled, but they liked her and asked her to sing with them. The piano player was named Stanley and they became really good friends. I liked him, too. He was funny.

Bill had some boy friends, but I liked them better than she did. One of them was especially nice, and every time he came to take her out to dinner he'd bring me a present, a really nice present, but that didn't last very long. He got to liking her so much that Bill couldn't stand him. Then she went to the company Christmas party at the John Marshall Hotel with a whole crowd of people from work. Of course, she had to sing. This man from Raleigh was there. His name was Mr. Williams. He was over all the stations in North Carolina and Virginia. Bill said he really was nice, and he seemed to really like her. She said he probably was married, 'cause he was sort of old. Anyway, at least he looked like a man and she was glad she met him. They got to be pretty good friends, every time he came to Richmond he'd go up to her office and visit with her. He invited her out to dinner several times, but she never would go. She liked him though. She did go out with several other men, but she really didn't like any of them.

On Saturdays when she didn't have to work, she and Mammy and I would go shopping, and we'd always have lunch at Miller and Rhoads Tea Room. That was our favorite place.

On Sundays Bill would take me out to Byrd Park and we'd have the best time. She'd rent a paddle boat and we'd ride around all over the lake. Once we got stranded right beneath the fountain and we couldn't move. We just sat there laughing and getting drenched. It was so funny. Finally, somebody turned off the fountain, and we were able to paddle out. If it was raining and we couldn't go to the park we'd go to the movies.

Lots of weekends we'd go to Roanoke Rapids, it was only about 70 miles from Richmond, to see Ann and Bobby.

Bobby had opened his practice there when he finished school in Chicago. We loved to visit them. They had two little girls my age and we always had the best time. Mama and Ann would go horse back riding. They had a stable and horses and everything. Sometimes we'd all go over to Littleton and spend the day. Littleton was not but 15 miles from Roanoke Rapids, but Ann said she never went unless Bill was there. Ann and Bill really loved each other. They loved to talk about when they lived in San Francisco and about when they lived in Littleton and all their aunts and uncles who were living then. I heard about them so much that I really felt like I knew them. I remember I used to say that someday when I grew up I was gonna write a book about them.

Every summer Bill would take me to Wilmington to see Aunt Kingsland. I loved to go there. She had two little girls, too, Susan and Kingsland Alston. I couldn't say Kingsland Alston, so I called her 'King Kong". We thought that was so funny. King Kong and I were close to the same age and we were really close cousins. My Uncle Howard was always playing tricks on us. One day we went to the movies and saw 'The Mummy.' Well, we were really scared just thinking about it, and do you know what Uncle Howard did? We were so scared we couldn't go to sleep that night, and he could hear us talking. Well, he wrapped a sheet around himself and knocked on the door, and all of a sudden the door opened and there he was, the Mummy! He said if we didn't stop talking and go to sleep he was coming back to get us. It just about scared us to death, but we did stop talking. We didn't know 'til the next morning at breakfast that it was Uncle Howard. I never will forget that night.

Bill would go back to Richmond and then in about two or three weeks she'd come back to get me. Sometimes Aunt Kingsland and Uncle Howard would take me back. It was always fun though, but I was always glad to get back home to Bill and Mammy and Da.

When I was five years old Bill wrote to my other grandmother, because one of the girls in her office told her it wasn't right for her to not know where her grandchild was. Well, one night about a week later the door bell rang. Bill was getting dressed to go out to dinner with Jerry Jarrette, (I think she really did like him.) Da was out of town, and Mammy and I were just about ready to sit down to supper. I was helping Bill get ready for her date, so I went with her to answer the door. We thought it was gonna be Jerry, but it wasn't. It was my daddy Bob! Well, Bill was speechless! But I knew right away who it was.

My Daddy Bob was big and tall, and he was just as good looking as Bill told me he was. He probably WAS the handsomest man in the whole world.

Well, Bill was in a state of shock. First of all, I had to go to the door when Jerry came and tell him that she wasn't feeling well and couldn't go out with him that night. Mammy was just flabbergasted when she saw him, too. Mammy was nice to him though. She made him sit down and eat supper with us.

He stayed in Richmond about three weeks and it was wonderful. It was almost like we had been with him all the time. Right off the bat I loved him just like I loved Bill. He had a pretty new car and he took us everywhere. It was so much fun. Bill had to go to work, of course, and when she did he'd pick me up at school (kindergarten) and take me to get ice cream. Sometimes we'd go to see a movie. Then when Bill got off work we'd go to pick her up and later we'd all go out to supper. Sometimes Mammy would invite him to eat with us. Bob thought Mammy was a real good cook.

Bill was really happy, but like she told you, he was married to somebody else. Her name was Chris. She called Bill everyday, even at work. She even called Mr. Wynne, Bill's boss. Well, Bill told her and Mr. Wynne did, too, that she

202

couldn't do anything about him being in Richmond, that she hadn't even known he was coming.

Daddy Bob told Bill that he didn't love Chris; that we were his family. But Bill told him that we could never stay together again as long as he was married to Chris.

And then he left. I never will forget that day. Bill was so sad, I was, too. Even Mammy missed him, I think. After a while, though, things got back to normal. Jerry Jarrett was mad because we were so nice to him when he was there, and because she had stood HIM up.

After a while Bill started dating Jerry again and then guess what? Daddy Bob just walked in one day. He didn't even knock, just opened the door and came in. My Da was really mad, and Mammy was, too. Daddy Bob said he had left Chris and wanted us to go back to Houston with him, but we didn't. I think Bill really wanted to, but she was trying to be sensible. He didn't even have a job. He just wanted us back. After that we didn't hear from him for a long time.

Jerry Jarrett got mad all over again, but he was even madder with my Daddy Bob. Da was really mad, too. They said that it just wasn't right for him to keep upsetting her life. Bill, though, was always just so glad to see him, and so was I.

When I was nine years old Bill went to New York. She wanted to look for a coat for me. She had one pictured in her mind and she hadn't been able to find one in Richmond. The real reason she went though, was because she wanted to see Mr. Lipset, the agent they had gotten for her when she was there before. She didn't really even know if he'd remember her, 'cause it had been over eleven years since she had seen him. To tell you the truth she really wondered if she was too old to sing up there but singing was still the only thing she really wanted to do.

Well, she found my coat right away and then she called Mr. Lipset. He remembered her all right. He told her to come straight to his office. She did, and he told her that if she would move to New York she could be singing all the time, and making good money. Said she was just what they were looking for. She went back to Richmond then. When she found out how easy it would be she didn't want to do it anymore.

Stanley, the piano player, wanted her to go to Miami with him. He kept trying to convince her how wonderful it would be. Said they could work in all the best clubs. Finally he talked her into it. She gave her notice and quit her job. Then the night before she was to leave I talked her out of going. I told her if she wouldn't go we could get our own apartment and I would cook supper for her every night. I just begged her not to go and she didn't. Stanley really got mad, he went on anyway, but Bill didn't.

I told you Bill had quit her job and they had already hired somebody to take her place. They told her that as soon as they had an opening they'd call her. She went back to the employment office and this time they sent her to AAA, the Triple A Motor Club. It was the first time they had ever hired anybody that didn't have a college education, but they liked her. She said she had never had to take so many tests and they had asked her about a million questions. So she went to work there and had worked there for several weeks before they found out she didn't know how to drive. Well, they were horrified!!!! They had asked her every question imaginable except, Do you know how to drive? They were going to make her learn to drive. They wanted to keep her, but she couldn't keep telling people which roads to take and telling them how to get through cities all over the United States if she didn't even know how to drive. So they were getting ready to give her driving lessons when the people from Trailways called her back.

Mammy and Da were moving to Raleigh, but Bill and I stayed in Richmond. We shared a house with the nicest woman and her little boy. He was my age, and he knew all the children in the neighborhood and we had the best time. Betty, the woman, was so nice and she and Bill really enjoyed each other. She didn't work like Bill, so she was home all day. She was always thinking up surprises and adventures. She and Bill became really good friends and we were always doing something interesting.

Bill really wanted to be singing, though, and Stanley kept calling and trying to make us go to Florida. He was in Vero Beach then and he said the manager of a beautiful club out on the Indian River was interested in hiring them and that would be a wonderful place to work. I could tell she was dying to go, like I've said before, the only thing she wanted to do was sing. Finally, I told her that if that was what she really wanted to do it would be all right with me.

I really didn't want to leave Richmond. I loved my school and my friends, but Bill was determined to go. So she gave her notice at work again. They did NOT want her to quit, she was very good at what she did, and they told her that if she quit this time they wouldn't be able to take her back. That was because the station had become a union station, and that was one of their rules. Bill hated the union and wouldn't join it, which was one of the reasons she wanted to leave.

206

So she took me to stay with Mammy and Da 'til she could send for me. The day before she left she got me a white Persian kitten. She thought that would make it easier for me. It didn't though, I loved Richmond.

Vero Beach ♪

Back to Me

This is really hard for me to even write about, for I have never forgiven myself for doing this. Jennie didn't want to go to Florida; she didn't want to leave Richmond. She liked her school, she had made some nice friends and she liked it there. (I'd give anything in the world if I had stayed in Richmond) I thought that she'd make friends anywhere we happened to be, that I'd be making more money, and I knew I'd be happier singing.

So I went to Vero Beach. Stanley was already there. He had a place lined up for us to audition, which we did, and the owner hired us. It was a beautiful club which was located out on the Indian River. I found a little apartment out at the beach, and called Mama and told her to bring Jennie. The day they arrived our job fell through. Stanley, who REALLY had 'delusions of grandeur', went out to see the owner of the club and demanded that he get a white baby grand piano, said we couldn't work unless we had one.

Well, the manager told him that if that was the case we just couldn't work. I could have murdered Stanley. Honestly, I was so mad!

So, to make a long story short there was nothing to do but go home. Daddy and Mama were living just outside of Raleigh, and that's where we ended up going. I couldn't afford to go back to Richmond and start all over, because I had spent all my money on that wild goose chase.

And so begins another phase of my life.

When we first moved to Raleigh Mama and Daddy lived in a little suburb called Garner. Garner was a just a small village then, located about 8 miles east of Raleigh.

Daddy took me into Raleigh to the Employment Office the first day we got there, and I got a job at Patterson Travel Service as a Travel Consultant. I really did enjoy that job. I liked the Patterson's and I liked the people who worked there. I liked the clients as well.

I had to ride the bus back and forth to work every day. The bus got to Raleigh about an hour before I had to be at work, so I would go in the coffee shop at the Bus Terminal and have a cup of coffee to pass the time. One morning I saw a man I had known in Richmond. His name was Mr. Williams, and he was an executive with Carolina Coach Co. and was over the Richmond office. (Remember, Jennie told you about him when I was in Richmond.) He recognized me and came over to talk to me. I thought he was very nice. He wanted to know why I hadn't applied for a job with his company. I told him I had a job I liked very much. To make a long story short, practically every morning when I'd go in the coffee shop he'd be there. Sometimes the manager of the station would be with him, and they both tried to talk me into coming to work there. They finally offered me quite a bit more money than I was making at Patterson's, and I couldn't refuse.

So I went back to work for Trailways. Mama never did like for me to work at a bus station, especially not then, the world was beginning to change, but I had to make as much money as I could, and I really wasn't trained to do anything. Anyway, it wasn't so bad. Actually there were some very nice people working there, some characters, too. I'll get to that later. I found out we aren't always able to do what we want to do.

One of the things Mama instilled in me was, that what ever happens, good or bad, no matter how good, no matter how bad, to not be changed because of it, to take it in stride. Another thing was, that one must always be true to one's self, to not be swayed by others, to not be changed by circumstances, and to always do what felt right.

Homer Drye (Briar Hopper) had gone to Raleigh straight from our Briar Hopper days, and he was still Homer Briar Hopper. He had his own show on WMFD-TV, the ABC affiliate, and later on WRAL-TV. He also had a Country-Western night club.

212

Homer was married and had a little boy. I had come down from Richmond several times to be a guest on his TV show. When he found out I was in Raleigh he immediately wanted me to appear as a regular on his show. I did for a while, but it came on EARLY in the morning and I was just not cut out for that kind of show, although I really appreciated the fact that he wanted me. I liked Ethel, his wife, and Jennie baby-sat with his little boy some. I worked with Homer for a while, he took his band to Fort Bragg often to play at the main Officer's Club, and I always went with him and sang with his band.

I did very little singing, other than that, in Raleigh. My kind of music was on the way out. When Elvis Presley appeared on the scene, music changed. I saw him the first time he appeared on Ed Sullivan's show. There have been a few country singers that I truly do like, Eddy Arnold and Jim Reeves, Dottie West and Bonnie Guitar. I suppose there have been others, but to tell you the truth I just don't listen to any of the country radio stations. Blues, that's my music. Thank goodness, I have lots of Tapes and CDs of the kind of music I like. And I have Digital TV music.

I wrote to Bob's mother and told her we were in Raleigh, and the next thing I knew, guess what? You're right. I looked up one day while I was at work, and there he was. I always loved him, and I was always so happy to see him, but now it was like you might love a favorite brother. I knew it was hopeless. I had accepted that fact, and it was almost like I couldn't feel anything, anymore. I told you that Mama said I'd have been better off if I had just died when Bob left. You know, in a way she was right. Part of me, the real me did die when he left. I never really got over it, and I couldn't understand it. I never will understand it. There was so much good in Bob, I could see it, even if others couldn't. His mother blamed a lot of the way he acted on the war. She said he was the best, the most dependable little boy imaginable.

He was a real hero, you know. He was in the worst of the war in the Pacific, the battles of Tarawa and Guadalcanal and was badly wounded receiving two Purple Hearts and two Presidential Citations. His helmet and Machine Gun are, or were, in the museum in Washington. And he was so young; he was only 17 when he volunteered.

War is such a horrible thing anyway. I don't understand how anybody could not be changed. He didn't talk a lot about it, sometimes though he'd tell me a little bit and you could tell how much it hurt him to even think about it, and he was so badly wounded. He stayed in the hospital 15 months. So, I've never really blamed Bob, he suffered so much, and we were both so young. I blame myself too, I was so impractical. It took me a long time to grow up. It took us both a long time to grow up. I just wish we could have grown up together.

I was always so thankful I had Jennie. She made up for everything I lost. I used to tell myself that as long as I had her nothing else really mattered, but I was always so worried that something might happen to her. It was like I almost felt that maybe I couldn't have anything I REALLY wanted, anymore. Everything that happened before, all the good life I had known seemed almost like a dream.

Mr. Williams started showing up every morning when it was time for my break if he was in town, and then he'd be back at lunch, and again for my afternoon break. I liked him at first, he was very nice looking, but my goodness, he must have been in his forties, besides that, he was married. To tell the truth, it was sort of embarrassing. Then when I was waiting for the bus in the mornings he'd drive up and take me to work. He always asked me to go to dinner with him, and I finally told him I never was going to go anywhere with him. I really began to not like him very much after he started liking me so much.

Everybody started teasing me about him, and I would laugh about it and let them listen in when he called me. Well, this went on for months. Then he told me his wife had left, he said they'd just been married in name only, anyway.

Of course, I told Mama all about it, and she thought it was funny, too. Every night when I got home from work she'd want to hear the next 'episode' of my soap opera. Mama told me though, that maybe I ought to go out to dinner with him, that maybe he really was a nice man and that I should be looking for somebody who would take care of Jennie and me.

Then all of a sudden he didn't come around so often, and when he did he was sort of aloof. To tell you the truth I liked him a whole lot better this way, and I even wondered why he had changed. It didn't occur to me that maybe he'd heard about the way I laughed at him. Then I began to worry that maybe he HAD heard, or even if maybe he'd met somebody else he liked better. Aren't human beings funny? Anyway, I began to look forward to seeing him, and when, after several weeks, he asked me to dinner I was only too glad to say, yes.

When Bob came that first time it made Mr. Williams mad, he said Bob shouldn't keep turning up like that. He had messed my life up, and that he should just leave me alone now. I suppose he was right. Every time he came I knew he wasn't going to stay, but when he left there was always this terrible let down. I knew there would never be anybody to take his place,

216

so I never really looked for anybody else. Maybe I should have tried harder; maybe my life would be easier today. I don't know. I just knew I loved him still, but I also knew it was hopeless. And you know what? I never really blamed Bob. He hurt himself just as much as he hurt us, because he really wanted us, he just didn't know how to keep us. That is what his sister said, not long ago. He was never really happy again after we separated. It is so sad. People really have a way of messing up their lives. But I should have been stronger. I should have grown up sooner before it was too late, before it didn't matter anymore. I'm all grown up now, but now it's too late. No, I don't blame him, anymore than I blame myself.

I was in my mid thirties then. Slowly my self confidence came back and like always I decided it was time for me to start singing again. One day, on a whim, I called Mr. Johnson in Myrtle Beach and asked him about coming to work for him. He said to come on down and let him see me and we'd talk about it. I hadn't seen him since I'd worked at the Flamingo in Charlotte, and that was ten years ago.

So I went to Myrtle Beach and saw him, and he was really nice. I was always, just a little bit, more than a little bit, in awe of him. He had the kind of eyes that could see right through you, you know, gambler's eyes, I guess. I always felt like he could see inside my head and see what I was thinking. Anyway, he hired me as soon as I sang one song and told me to come to work in two weeks.

This was going to be a completely different kind of job for me. I would be the hostess and sing with the orchestra, two songs each set, and the pay was good, so I quit my job and went to Myrtle Beach.

Well, this turned out to be a REALLY different kind of job! In the first place; he wasn't there to meet me when I arrived. This man I had never seen before came up and asked me if I was Billie Burton. He introduced himself as 'Turk' and said that Mr. Johnson had been called out of town, He had a club in Miami and his partner down there had called him, there was some sort of emergency. Anyway, he said the band was out at the club waiting to rehearse with me, and that Mr. Johnson had instructed him to get a hotel room for me, that he would be back in town in two days and then he would find a place for me to stay.

So he drove me out to the club, and sure enough, the band was waiting. It was a good band, too, and I enjoyed rehearsing with them. Two girls were out there; they were nice looking girls and seemed very friendly. They told Turk it would be foolish for me to go to a hotel, that I was welcome to share their apartment until Mr. Johnson got back. Turk told them "no", that Mr. Johnson had already made reservations for me at a hotel. I couldn't understand why he was so opposed to my staying with them. I thought it was silly for him to have to pay for a hotel when they had invited me to stay with them, so to make a long story short, I went home with them, and I thought they were the nicest girls in the world.

That night when I was dressing to go to work they practically dressed me. I mean one of them fixed my hair, the other one made me up. They even MADE me wear some of their beautiful jewelry. They really acted like professionals.

I took a taxi to work and when I walked in everybody was so nice. I was just a little unsure of my self, because I had never worked as a hostess before, and I really didn't know what I was supposed to do.

Turk told me the main thing was to watch the door. The door was kept locked; there was a two way mirror in the top half of the door. I could see out, but the people who came up to the door from the outside couldn't see in. If they rang the door bell then I was to look at them and if they looked presentable I could let them in. If not, I was to call Turk and he would come and talk to them and turn them away. The ladies had to be dressed in pretty summer dresses. The men had to wear a shirt, tie and nice looking sport jacket or a nice suit. No shorts were allowed. If they looked all right then I showed them to a table and got a waitress for them.

I found out that very night that this club did not adhere to any rules set down by the state of South Carolina. (That was primarily the reason the door was kept locked.) In the first place, we had an open bar and South Carolina laws prohibited that. In the second place, it was a gamblers paradise, unlike anything in this part of the United States.

When it was time for me to sing Turk would come and take over my duties at the door. Well, it was FUN! The night just flew by. I got lots of applause, they really seemed to like me, and it seemed almost like it used to. I really enjoyed it.

This was a very popular place, frequented by very nice looking people, by most of the politicians, judges, and other people of authority in the state. Well, about 12:30 when I answered the door and looked out, there were these two GORGEOUS girls and two very nice looking men. I opened the door and let them in, and I couldn't believe it. I hadn't even recognized them. They were my room-mates! That afternoon when I had met them they had just looked like wholesome young girls. They weren't even wearing any makeup and now!

220

Wow! They looked like show girls. Dressed to the nines, lots of make-up, and they were BEAUTIFUL! I couldn't get over it.

Turk took me back to the girl's apartment after the club closed that night. He told me he didn't feel good about my staying with those girls, that Mr. Johnson was gonna be very upset with him AND with me. Anyway, when he put me out he said for me to come to his restaurant, which was only a block away, for breakfast. I told him I'd see him then. I got undressed and watched television while I waited for my apartment mates to come home. I watched a whole movie and they still hadn't come home, so finally I just went to bed. I slept 'til about 11 the next morning and when I woke up there was no sign of my room-mates. I was really kind of worried.

Somebody knocked on the door and when I answered, it was Flo. She was this very pretty woman who was the black jack dealer at the club. I had met her the night before. She told me she lived downstairs and invited me to come have coffee with her. She waited while I got dressed and then we went down to her apartment. She told me she wanted me to stay with her 'til Mr. Johnson got back in town. I told her I couldn't do that, and that I was very worried about the girls, because they hadn't come home last night, and I was afraid that something might have happened to them.

Well, she told me not to worry, that she felt sure they were all right, but that she was sure Mr. Johnson would not like it at all when he found out I was staying with them. I couldn't understand what all the 'to do' was about, and I told her I thought it would be terribly impolite if I just moved for no reason, so I thanked her for the coffee and went back upstairs and my room mates were home!

I was SO relieved! I told them I had been terribly worried. They just laughed and said there was no reason for me to worry, that they had been to a party, and it had lasted all night. I can't even remember their names now, but I remember them VERY well. Anyway, they said to put on my bathing suit and come with them out on the beach. I told them "no", that I had promised Turk I'd come to his restaurant for breakfast. They told me where they'd be and said to come on after I had eaten.

The food was pretty good at Turks, I enjoyed it. He came over and sat with me for a while, and started telling me again that he just didn't feel good about my staying with those girls. I thought he was crazy, and kept trying to tell him how nice they were.

After I finished eating I just went on back to the apartment. I was really kind of tired 'cause I hadn't slept much the night before, and too, I wanted to write to Jennie.

The next night the same thing happened, they came to the club and then, they didn't come home. I wasn't too worried though, I thought they had just probably gone to another party. I slept well that night.

Well, the next morning I was up at Turks eating breakfast again, and the waitress came and said that Mr. Johnson was outside in his car and wanted me to come out there. I was a little scared, because I certainly didn't want him to be mad with me. He was sitting in his car, and he leaned over and opened the door, and he said (even before I had a chance to say hello to him.) "Billie Burton", get in this car," and I said "Mr. Johnson I haven't finished my breakfast yet." He said, "Get in, you can finish it later, you are moving, young lady, and I mean now. Come on, get in." So I got in, and he was mad! He said "Do you know, no I don't think you have sense enough to know that those girls you're living with are prostitutes! Hell, they could be arrested anytime, and you'd be arrested, too, if you're with them. I've known you since you were a little girl, and I'm not going to let you come down here and get mixed up with that kind. If I'd been here they wouldn't have been out there anyway. I don't allow them in my place." Well, I was really shocked. I didn't have any idea that they were prostitutes. They certainly didn't look like I thought prostitutes would look.

Anyway, he took me to their apartment, (thank goodness, they weren't there) and waited till I packed my things, and then he took me to Paul's Guest House. He had already gotten me a room there. He said that was all I needed, that there were several good restaurants near by, and I could eat at the club at night.

Wouldn't you think that after working in clubs and cocktail lounges all those years, not to mention a Bus Terminal, for goodness sakes, that I ought to know a lot more about this world than I did? Honestly though, I don't believe that I was ever exposed to that side of life. If I was, I certainly didn't know it. Maybe I was just dumb. He told me that under no circumstances was I to ever get in touch with them again. That he'd send me home if I did. I told him that I ought to at least call them and thank them for their hospitality. He said, "No way," that he was sure they'd understand.

Anyway, I kept working for him, and believe me, that was an experience. I met all kinds of interesting people. I got to know those people and I liked them, but I never was a part of them. Seems to me, that most of my life, I've just been an

224

observer. All those years on the band stand I'd get up and sing my songs and then I'd sit down and smile and enjoy the music and watch the dancers and the people. At intermission, sometimes, I'd sit with people, but mostly, I liked to sit with the men in the band, and it would make me mad with people who just insisted that I come to their table. Well, though, I met some really nice people.

Those people in Myrtle Beach, however, that was a different world. I loved to watch the people playing black jack, and sometimes I'd go in the game room and watch the people gambling.

Mr. Johnson was one of a kind. He traveled with an entourage. Lots of men worked for him, most of them were professional gamblers. He went to Las Vegas several times a year. He called it Vegas. He had other clubs, one in Southern Pines (or Pinehurst) I can't remember. He had come to the beach during prohibition, (I think he was a bootlegger.) and had acquired lots and lots of land. He may have had connections with the underworld, maybe, I certainly don't know. I'll say this for him, he was a gentleman. I never felt safer anywhere than when I worked for Mr. Johnson. All those people who worked for him couldn't have been nicer to me. I got to know his family. He and his wife, Peggy, had several children. They had a pretty home out on the ocean, a swimming pool and everything. Mr. Johnson didn't live there. He had an apartment upstairs over the club. He and his wife had been separated a long time. She was a pretty woman, and in a way I think he still loved her. I found out he had a mistress, it was Flo, the Black Jack dealer, I liked her, too. He loved his children. I spent Easter weekend with Peggy and the children, and he came out there early Easter morning with HUGE Baskets, very expensive ones I think, I've never seen any so pretty. I suppose, if I had to name my most unforgettable character it would be Mr. Johnson. He never treated mc like anything but a child, and he looked out for me too. He also didn't think I was very bright, I'm afraid. He said I was the most gullible person he had ever seen.

I could write a whole book about the people I got to know down there. There was a beautiful "belly dancer" who had the whitest skin and the blackest hair, and when she danced with all those colorful veils the whole room smelled like her perfume. I got to know all the gamblers, and you know they were really nice to me.

One night I looked out the door and it looked like about a million policemen were standing out there. Well, that scared me to death. I ran and told Turk, and he came to the door and looked. Turk told me to just calm down, then he went with me into the bar and told me to sit down on a bar stool. Then he called one of the gamblers to come in and sit down beside me and he told the bar tender to give me a drink. He said, "Now you just sit here and pretend to be a customer, and you'll be fine." I was so nervous I picked up the drink and took a big gulp and it was SCOTCH! I had never even tasted it before, and that was really a shock to my system, let me tell you. Anyway, all these uniformed men came in and went behind the bar and took all the alcohol, (and there was a lot of it) then one of them got up to the microphone and said "Ladies and Gentlemen, this club has just been raided by SLED (State Law Enforcement Division?) and will be closed. We ask that all patrons please vacate the premises." Well, I thought I was ruined! About that time Turk came and told Haskell, the gambler to take JoRee, one of the cocktail waitresses, and me over to the 19th Hole, (another of Mr. Johnson's clubs) and wait 'til he called. So that's what he did. JoRee wasn't even scared. She was a darling girl, a student at Peace College in Raleigh and her father was a lawyer for SLED. She said not to worry. It was all a hoax, Mr. Johnson knew they were coming and all that stuff they had carried out, they had put in Mr. Johnson's van. I had kind of wondered why none of the politicians that were usually out there were not there that night. It was because they knew. About an hour later Turk called and told us to come on back.

227

I learned a lot in Myrtle Beach. One thing I learned was that some of the people who were considered the worst were really the best, and that some of the people who were considered the best were not really very good at all.

The day after Labor Day <u>everything</u> closed! All the clubs closed, most of the restaurants, everything, so I went back to Raleigh. Mr. Williams, who by now was my very good friend, was instrumental in getting me a job in the auditing department at Queen City Trailways in Charlotte, so again, I went back to Charlotte.

No Grudges ♫

You may have gathered by now that I don't hold grudges, neither thank goodness, do most of the people who remained my friends through these many years. One of those people was Mrs. Thomas. I felt a kinship to her when Clarence first introduced us, and even though that friendship was sorely tested when she and Clarence did their best to send Bob packing, I couldn't remain mad with her. In hindsight, I can see, certainly, their reasons for trying to break us up. Mrs. Thomas no longer had Royal Oaks. That was a big responsibility, I know. She had bought a very nice home out beyond Mercy Hospital and she invited me to stay with her until I got settled. I wanted Jennie to come as soon as possible, so I was looking for a place for us. Mrs. Thomas had been telling me for months that a girl from Littleton had moved in down the street and wanted me to please call her the next time I came for a visit. I was curious about her and wanted to meet her, as well. Littleton is a very small town, and you just don't meet people from there very often, so I called and she invited me for coffee, and I went down to see her. He name was Betsy Thornton Medlin, I hadn't known her, because I am older than she is, and I left Littleton when I was in the fourth grade and she hadn't even started in the first grade yet.

Well, right off the bat, we became fast and lasting friends. We established the fact on that first visit that we were cousins, for we shared the same ancestor, Gideon Macon, also we knew so many of the same people, and it was like I had known her forever. She had a little girl, Macon, younger than Jennie, but they grew to adore each other, and George, her husband was one of the nicest people I have ever known. Betsy remains to this day, one of my closest friends and confidants.

So, I stayed with Mrs. Thomas again until I found a place for Jennie and me to live. The place I found was on Croyden Road, a beautiful street off of Queens Road West. Actually, Carolyn found this place, and it was quite near to them on Selwyn Ave. It was a boarding house just for women. Mrs. Linker, the proprietor, was very selective and only had four guests besides Jennie and me. There were five bedrooms upstairs. Each of the women had a large private room, and I was delighted that she allowed Jennie and me to share a room. The food was delicious, the ladies who lived there were lovely, and all seemed to like Jennie and me very much. As I said, Carolyn and Walter lived nearby, and Walter came every morning and took Jennie to school along with their two daughters. I enjoyed being back in Charlotte. Working in an Auditing Office was not really my 'cup of tea', but then office work of any kind was grueling labor to me. Actually, it wasn't so bad. I really liked my boss, he was funny. Mr. Williams came often, (he was over that station, as well) and he always took me out to dinner. Charlie was still in Charlotte, and we saw lots of him.

We stayed with Mrs. Linker for several months. Later I found a nice apartment and I was pretty content the way things were, but Jennie never really liked Charlotte. Charlotte is a 'clicky' town, especially the schools, and Jennie missed her friends in Raleigh. I was so stupid. School had never mattered that much to me, there just wasn't time for me to have friends, what with singing and all. But with Jennie, it did matter, and I am so sorry that I didn't understand. I failed her in so many ways and I'll never forgive myself. I just loved her with all my heart and I thought that as long as we had each other that was all that mattered.

We went back to Raleigh every two or three weeks to see Mama and Daddy. They came to spend one Christmas with us. We had been in Charlotte a little over two years when Daddy called one night and said that Mama was in the hospital. We went right away, and she was quite ill. She recovered though, thank goodness. After that, Jennie refused to go back to Charlotte. So she stayed with Mama and Daddy and I began to go home almost every weekend.

About a year later they called me at work from the Raleigh Terminal and offered me more money if I'd come back to work for them. So I went back, but this time I just could hardly stand it. After about a month I called Mr. Johnson in Myrtle Beach again. I hadn't sung in a long time. Rock and Roll was everywhere. It was inconceivable to me, still is, the appeal that kind of music had and has for so many people. Mr. Johnson didn't like it either, and he told me to come on back. I asked him if I could bring Jennie; she was seventeen then. Most of the cocktail waitresses were college students, and I thought Jennie would enjoy living at the beach and making lots of money, because it was amazing, the money cocktail waitresses made. All you had to be was pretty, and Jennie was certainly that. Very tall and slender with shoulder length auburn hair and huge green eyes. It didn't occur to me, that that might not be a good environment for Jennie. I had worked in so many clubs in my young life, and it hadn't effected me.

At first Jennie thought it was great. Every night, after we got home from work, I'd help her count her money and it was amazing how much she made. Lots of people we knew came to Myrtle Beach to see us, and it was always fun to see everybody and go out to eat with them. There are so many wonderful seafood restaurants in Myrtle Beach. Jennie would get up early every morning and go out on the beach; she met lots of people her age and seemed to be having wonderful time. Jennie, though, was in love with a boy in Raleigh. He came several times to see her. When he was there, she didn't want to go to work. This made Mr. Johnson mad. This, in turn, made Jennie mad, so she went back to Raleigh several times to see Mama and Daddy, she said. I think, really, that was just a good excuse. Anyway, finally, she just went back to Raleigh to stay. I stayed on 'til the end of summer. They called me, on Labor Day, from Trailways in Raleigh and asked me to come back.

When Jennie was eighteen she went to New York with twin girls that she knew. For several months I didn't even know where she was. I nearly lost my mind. Finally she called; she was working in a place call Pal Joey's. After several months she called and asked if she could come home. Of course she could come home; I couldn't wait to see her. I'll never forget how she looked when she got home, she looked like Twiggy, very tall and paper thin, even had Twiggy's hairdo. She should have been a model. She only stayed with me a few months, and then she moved in with some girls she knew. She went to NC State for a while. She was so smart, I wonder sometime, was she too smart. Anyway she got a job at the Hilton Hotel, which was next to the State campus, as a bartender. I called her every day, but I didn't see her all that often. That little girl who had loved me so much just didn't have much time for me anymore. That is a phase that they all go through, I suppose.

All this time I hadn't heard from Bob. I saw a lot of Mr. Williams. We talked about getting married. So he made me call Bob's mother to find out where Bob was, because he wanted me to get a divorce. I finally did call her and learned that Bob was living with her again, and he had been very sick. Bob started calling me and writing me again. He begged me to come out to Texas, he told me he was dying, and that he couldn't die without seeing me again. This time Mama and Daddy REALLY tried to talk me out of going. So did Mr. Williams. He said Bob was just saying that to keep me from marrying him. That all I had to do was divorce him. I guess I don't have to tell you that I went. Bob was sick, he was thin, and didn't really look like he did before, but he was still handsome. I stayed for a week. Houston had become a huge city. Bob and I went back to Hermann Park one day and spent the day, just like we used to do. The Zoo there is wonderful. I enjoyed being with him again, but I knew I had to come back home. His mother and his aunt both told me not to let him talk me into staying. He begged me to stay, when I left he was inconsolable, just cried like a baby. It was so sad, I loved him still, and I know he loved me, but I knew it was hopeless, and I knew, too, that that was the last time I'd ever see him. He wrote often, and called many times.

He told me he was gaining weight and felt much better and was coming to Raleigh. He never made it, though. Mr. Williams never really forgave me for going out there. Oh, we were still friends, but he didn't mention marriage anymore. He said I still loved Bob.

Mama and Daddy, by this time, were living in Wake Forest, a small town not far from Raleigh. One Monday morning, early, a neighbor of theirs called. They had been trying to reach me, but I had been out of town. Anyway she said that Daddy had had a stroke and was in the hospital, and that Mama was just so upset. So I called and talked to Mama and told her that we'd be out to get her so she could stay with me while Daddy was in the hospital. Then I called Mr. Williams and asked him to take me out to get her.

So we brought her home to my apartment. Daddy seemed to be doing fairly well. The stroke had just affected his speech. Other than that he seemed all right. His appetite was good. Mama, though, was just not feeling very well. She started having these little spells, I'd be talking to her and all of a sudden she'd close her eyes. She said everything just seemed to turn black and then she'd be all right. Too, most days when I'd be ready to go to see Daddy, she didn't feel like going, and that wasn't like her, at all. Mama was still beautiful, but for the past year she just hadn't been herself.

I had to work, but I'd call home every two or three hours to check on her, and I'd go home for lunch every day. One day, late in the afternoon, I called, and she said "Oh, Willie, please come home, I've fallen and nearly killed myself." I rushed home, and even before I opened the door I could hear Geronimo, my little dog, barking like crazy. She was lying on the bed and seemed to be in agony. I wanted to call an ambulance, but she wouldn't let me. She said she had gotten in the bathtub and when she got out and was going back to the bedroom she had fallen. The next day, Kingsland Alston, who was married and living nearby, came, and we made her go to the emergency room. They admitted her for tests. She and Daddy were on the same floor. Every night Daddy would wake up in the middle of the night and go around to Mama's room and sit with her. I had practically moved into the hospital. I had a cot in her room, and stayed there every night. One day I had gone home to feed Geronimo, and Daddy called and said the doctor had just talked to him and said that we'd never take Mama home again, that she had Arteriosclerosis, which is a fast moving hardening of the arteries. That was like a night mare. Nothing is worse than waiting for someone you love to die and still trying to be cheerful around them. Oh, it was awful! One night, toward the last, I had turned out the lights because I thought she was sleeping. I was sitting there in the dark when out of a clear blue sky, she said, "Willie", I said 'Yes, Mama?" She said, "Darling, you've got to take this in your stride, you've taken so much, but now you've got to take this, too. Just take it in your stride, and you'll be fine." It almost killed me, and I couldn't say anything. All I said was, "Yes mam, don't you worry." That was the only time she ever alluded to the fact that she knew she was dying. Daddy was so sad; he sat by her bed and patted her hand. Three days later she was gone. Kingsland was there, she had come the day before and had decided this time to spend the night, because she knew the end was near. I was almost asleep, I hadn't slept for weeks and I was so tired. I heard Kingsland's feet hit the floor and I asked her what was wrong. She said Mama had made a strange noise. We were beside her bed when she drew her last breath. For the first time in the five weeks that Mama had been in the hospital, Daddy hadn't woke up. So we waited 'til the next morning when the doctor came, and we went with him to Daddy's room to wake him and tell him. Dr. Allen cried when he told him. That was so sad. There is so much sadness in this world. Daddy lived for five more years, and never have I known anybody to be any more unhappy than he was.

They say we never grow up until our parents are gone. Even then, though I was chronologically certainly an adult, in some ways I was not very mature. If we live long enough, though, we have to face reality, and that can be very hard to do. The next years that ensued proved to be quite uneventful as far as I was concerned.

Mr. Williams, who I thought, had been my very good friend for many years, married a woman close to his age, the year after Mama died. If nothing else, that taught me to never depend on anybody again, for I had depended on him. Oh, he came back, very contrite, and said what a mistake he'd made, how much he loved me, blah, blah, blah. Finally I told him that if he really loved me to never call me again, to just leave me alone now, and he took me at my word. I've never heard from him again. Maybe the fact that I went back to Texas to see Bob had something to do with it, who knows; what I really think though, what I know, is that the woman he married was financially very well off.

The years went by; Jennie was the bartender at the Raleigh City Club, which was located on the top floor of the Sir Walter Hotel. She also was managing the Dinner Theater at the Sir Walter Hotel. Every week I'd go shopping with her for evening apparel to wear when she introduced the Dinner

Theater. And she was the Banquet Manager as well. She was so capable, everything she endeavored to do, she did well. She was very pretty, had a wonderful personality, and could talk to men on their own level. She was very well informed, as I've said before, any thing I wanted to know, I'd just ask Jennie. I just simply adored her, and I was so proud of her, she was the center of my world.

During this time, not too long after I moved back to Raleigh, Betsy and George moved to Raleigh. Betsy's father had died and had left her a great deal of land. A lot of this land was on Lake Gaston, a very large man made fresh water lake which came into being when the Roanoke River was dammed. George had the knowledge and the foresight to see that this land should be developed, and this proved to be a very good decision.

It became apparent to George, even before I realized it, that Jennie was drinking too much. The idea that Jennie would ever have a drinking problem had never occurred to me. As I said, I saw her most of the time in the day time, when we'd go shopping or to lunch. Sometimes at parties, I'd get mad at her for drinking, and she'd tell me that everybody drank at parties, and I shouldn't be such a 'stick in the mud.' I don't know; I just didn't dream that she drank like that very often. I began to worry though. Jennie adored George; he was really like a second father to her. I thought if anybody could make Jennie come to her senses it would be him. I knew she'd listen to him. Unfortunately though, George passed away quite suddenly. Jennie was devastated, as was I. George was a good friend. So, the only person that Jennie would listen to was gone.

Daddy was so sick, and I didn't want to worry him, for I knew he just wasn't able to help her. As it turned out, Daddy died just a month after George. And so begins the saddest, the most unbelievable period of my life.

Jennie ♫

Can you imagine how terrible it would be to watch the person who filled your life, the person who WAS your life, deliberately self-destruct? For that in essence, is what an alcoholic does. This beautiful, intelligent, good little girl found life so cruel, so unfair, that she was unable to cope without the most insidious of all drugs, alcohol. There is no possible way that I could ever understand, for alcohol for me was never the slightest temptation. I despise it. I have studied enough however, to know that this need is a cruel and deadly disease. It is one that can be arrested in some but not in all, no matter how hard they struggle to abstain. She tried so hard, so many times, but her need was too great. Jennie was quite artistic, and had an artist's sensitivity. I believe, basically, Jennie was terribly shy, and that alcohol bolstered her ego and gave her courage. Too, Jennie suffered many disappointments and alcohol became the crutch on which she leaned. It is impossible for me to understand why fate dealt my little girl such a cruel hand. No, it's not fair. But who can I blame? This is very hard for me to write about, for it dredges up things that I had forgotten; probably things that are best forgotten. She struggled for a long, long time. She tried so hard to stop, admitted herself for treatment many times. My darling little girl, my life. It almost kills me.

It was during this time, close to the beginning really, that she called me as I was fixing breakfast one Saturday morning and told me that Bob's sister had called and told her that Bob had passed away. It was a blow, even though it had been so long since we had heard from him. His was a sad life too, and a wasted life, for nobody had more potential than Bob. He was his own worst enemy. I'll always remember how it was when we were together. He caused me a lot of grief, but he also brought me the greatest happiness that I have ever known. It's because of these memories that I have been able stand the trouble I have known. I have known complete and utter happiness, I am thankful for that.

Jennie's health began to fail. I cannot even remember how many times she was hospitalized, how she suffered, how I suffered, for nothing is worse than to helplessly watch a loved one suffer. She quit drinking for a year and a half one time, went back to school and was doing so well and began to look like herself again. I was so proud of her. It didn't last though, nothing worked out right for her, and she just couldn't take it, not without this demon that was so readily available. And WHY didn't good things happen to her. I'll never understand. I see others now everyday that are not half as pretty, not nearly as smart, and I'll bet not half as good, but who, for some reason have found loving husbands and children. Why were they so blessed? Jennie loved children, she'd have been the best little mother. I try not to be bitter, but I'll never understand.

She came back to live with me. I was so glad to have her. I thanked God for her every day, many times every day. She was the focal point of my life. For a while she'd do o.k., and then she'd drink again; not while I was with her, she never drank while I was around, but I was working and had to go to bed fairly early, and after I'd go upstairs to bed, she'd drink. You wouldn't believe how many empty bottles I found, how many full bottles I found and poured down the sink, or how many crumpled brown paper ABC bags I found, under sofa cushions, in the most unlikely places, everywhere. I couldn't control it by not giving her money because she worked and she had her own money.

Alcohol is almost impossible to avoid. It's everywhere. It makes me so mad the way our hypocritical government fights tobacco, but you seldom hear anything against alcohol, and that kills more people and innocent people as well, and breaks up more homes, destroys more relationships than tobacco ever could. Another thing, they categorize alcoholics and drug addicts together, and there is no comparison. Alcohol is legal, it is accepted by society, and it's everywhere. Really, you have to explain why you don't drink. You're expected to drink. You're not a 'good sport' if you don't. 'Join the party, let your hair down, don't be a party pooper. Have a good time, enjoy yourself. You only go around once.' I've heard it all, and I can imagine how hard it must be, especially if you want a drink, to decline.

Another thing, they treat drug addicts in the same facilities as alcoholics, and it's in-excusable, it's wrong. Jennie nearly lost her life at Butner because of a drug addict. When I think about it, I can hardly stand it. I don't know how I DO stand it, and I am so furious with myself, for not being able to send her to a place that would truly have helped her. In these past years, however, I've heard of people who received treatment in the best places available, but yet were unable to quit. Alcohol is a demon, it takes hold and won't let go. And contrary to popular belief, it is not a sign of weakness, it's a disease as lethal, and as deadly as cancer. It can be arrested in some but not in all.

Things were not so bad all the time; I loved having her with me again. She was, by now, in her thirties, but to me she was always a child, always my most prized possession. I loved

244

her completely. I was obsessed by her. She was everything. Nobody knows how much I prayed, hoped against hope that she'd stop drinking. And when I first realized that she had a problem, I was so embarrassed, I lived in fear that people would find out. And I was so afraid, constantly afraid, that I'd lose her, and I would get so mad, so furious at her for destroying the one person in this world who was my reason for being in this world. So I fussed. Oh! How I wish I could take back some of the hateful things I said to her. I'd get so MAD! I just couldn't understand. You have to go through it, I suppose, to understand, but it's indescribable, it's awful.

Finally, she agreed to go to AA. I was so glad, so proud of her. I went to Alanon. I found this to be, to me at least, a very selfish thing, you were supposed to think mainly of yourself, to kick them out if need be, to go on with your life and to let them reach rock bottom, and 'maybe' then they'd straighten up and do right.

Almost immediately this woman who was a recovering alcoholic herself, took an interest in Jennie, and asked her to come and live with her and her husband. She told her that they would take her to meetings and help her to get back her self esteem. I was filled with gratitude to this woman, I thought what a wonderful thing, and I really thought this might be the answer. This proved to be a very short lived thing, in the first place Jennie was an extremely nice looking girl, and was very young to be going to AA. Several men, including the husband of the 'good Samaritan' who was helping her, made unwanted advances toward her and she quickly became disenchanted with the whole thing, as did I, with Alanon.

Finally, of her own accord, she agreed to go into a treatment center. Again, I was filled with optimism; this surely would be the answer, so I agreed to go to counseling for the time that she was in treatment. In order to get off the allotted time from my work I had to swallow my pride and tell my boss about Jennie's problem. My supervisor could not have been nicer or more understanding. The treatment center didn't prove to be very beneficial however. Oh, she quit for several months, but it didn't last. This is very hard for me to write about. All this time it was like being on a roller coaster. Things would go smoothly and up for a while, but then the bottom would fall out, and it would become a bottomless pit. And I was absolutely helpless to do anything to help her. Money, as well, was a tremendous item. She went many times to state and county facilities, which as far as I can tell, are worthless. In the first place they don't keep their patients long enough to really help them. Another thing, they mix them up with hardened criminals, for some criminals agree to go to treatment rather than go to jail. It's a nightmare. Jennie was so vulnerable, so easily hurt. Oh, it is such a shame!

Anyway, to get on with my story, my worst fears were realized. The dreaded phone call came about four o'clock one morning. She was in the hospital, and this time I knew would be the last time. And so I stood by her bed and watched her die. And I couldn't cry. Some things just hurt too much. It would be a blessed relief if I were able to break down and sob. I just had to take it. What else could I do? They, of course, called a code blue, but it took twenty minutes to bring her back and they told me her brain had probably been effected. I waited for the doctor to come early the next morning, and I told him to take her off the machine. To see her without that wonderful mind would have been almost worse than death. The doctor said he was going to do that anyway, because every cavity in her body was bleeding, and it was hopeless; that she would probably die within the next three or four hours. I couldn't go back in the room with her, I just couldn't. I wish now I had, but I just couldn't. Jennie, my Jennie, was already gone, and I just waited for her body to die. Kingsland and Mary Daniel and her husband, Eddy, were there with me, and we waited. I watched as Mary Daniel called the crematorium, and made arrangements, and I couldn't cry. My world had ended, all that mattered was gone, and still I couldn't cry. You see, I knew this day would come, and I had to get through it.

Her ashes were buried in Littleton; I put them in the ground myself, between the graves of Daddy and Mama's father, her great Grandpapa Bob Alston. Her little grave is surrounded by those of most of those dear people I wrote about in the beginning of this story. Her great, great grandparents and great, great, great grandparents are there as well.

I went back to work the following Monday. The show must go on. It was almost like a dream, I was apart from the whole thing and just watching. And it's been that way ever since. I watch the world, but I'm no longer a part of the world.

Three years before the end came Jennie had been hospitalized with liver failure, and had almost died. Miraculously, she recovered. The doctors told her that if she ever drank again it would kill her. (She'd been told that several times before.) Anyway, it was almost like a miracle, she didn't drink, she went to work, she went to school to be a computer programmer, made 4.0 in all her classes, and began to look like herself again; seemed to really be content. Oh, I was so happy. She wanted a computer, so though I really couldn't afford it, I bought her one. Back then they were pretty costly, very few people had one. It was like a really wonderful dream. My Jennie, the REAL Jennie had come back to me.

The following summer, late summer, Betsy invited both of us to visit her on Lake Gaston. Jennie really didn't seem to want to go, but I insisted, I thought a vacation would be good for her. So she went with Betsy earlier in the week, and Macon, Betsy's daughter was going to take me up there that weekend. Everything went according to plan and when Macon and I got there, Jennie seemed glad to see us. I developed a really bad headache, and went to bed early. Well, in the middle of the night, it really got bad, so I got up and went in the living room, Jennie was still up, and I asked her to bring me a glass of water so I could take an aspirin. When she came into my room I realized she'd been drinking. Well, it almost killed me!!!! I was so mad with her. I just couldn't believe it. When we went back to Raleigh she didn't drink anymore, to my knowledge, but I was always suspicious, so things were never really the same. On Valentine's Day, the next year, she started drinking again, and it was like the world had come to a screeching halt. My world just collapsed. Anyway, it went from bad to worse. She agreed to go back for treatment, but it just didn't help. One day I went home for lunch as I usually did, my office was just across the street, and Jennie was gone. She had taken her computer and the VCR I had given her for Christmas and had just disappeared. I found out later she had pawned them. I didn't hear from her then until a week later. She called and asked me to send her some money. She was in Atlantic Beach. I heard from her every week after that, some times two or three times a week. I got her a calling card, so she could call me. She'd always tell me she was not drinking, but sometimes I could tell she was. I just sort of gave up. Every time I'd hear from her, it was like a reprieve, she was still living, but I knew it couldn't last. There was nothing I could do. She was a grown woman, free to do what she saw fit to do, and she knew, smart as she was, she couldn't help but know, that she was killing herself, but alcohol was that important to her, more important to her than life itself. I begged her to come home, but she didn't want to do that, she said she was fine; she had met somebody and was going to get married. Once she did come home for a weekend, but she couldn't wait to go back. You know, if I could have, I'd have had her put in jail. I'd have done ANYTHING to get her away from this horrible alcohol. I do despise it!!!! I don't like to be around people who are drinking. I won't go to a cocktail party. I think it is the most evil, the worst thing in this world.

I was working for the State then, (can't remember if I told you) and had planned to retire and move back to Myrtle Beach. Music, still, was IT for me. When you sing jazz, you can always work, age doesn't really matter; in fact, it's almost an asset, because it's people like me who really know it. After Jennie died though, there was just no point in even trying, anymore. Too, my voice just seemed to have gone. It was almost like the real me was gone. Everything I'd hoped for, nothing mattered anymore. You go on living, but the spice of life is gone, like making a cake without vanilla; nothing to look forward to, ever again. Grief is a terrible thing.

I had never really liked Raleigh, so decided I might as well move back to Wilmington. Kingsland and her family were here, and Mary Daniel and Eddy had moved back when he retired. I thought as well, it wouldn't cost so much to live there. I thought too, that maybe I wouldn't miss Jennie so much in a new place. I never wanted to forget her, I used to worry that I might, but you don't forget. But it hurt so much. Everywhere I'd go, every time I went down town, it almost killed me. I tried so hard to take it, you know. Why was I left? I was so alone. Not lonely, I've never been lonely. I'm a self contained unit, I have always been perfectly content by myself, but now there was nobody but my self to even be concerned about. As long as there was the possibility that Jennie might call, then I was content to just stay at home and cook and read and listen to music and watch television and walk my little dog. I was perfectly happy to wait for her call. That was all I needed. But now there was nothing, she'd never call again; I'd never hear her voice again; now there was nothing in my life but emptiness. There was nothing left to hope for.

So I called Kingsland and told her I was coming back to Wilmington. She told me the most convenient place for me to live, that it is close to two good grocery stores and the Mall. I'm such an idiot; I've never learned to drive. When I was young and Jennie was still a little girl I couldn't have afforded a car. Bus service was pretty good back then. Besides, Daddy took me everywhere I needed to go. So, I called Mary Daniel, and she found me an apartment, and back again I came to Wilmington. I brought my little dog, Muffin and Jennie's cat, Twinkle.

For the first time since I was 12 years old (except when Jennie was a baby) I wasn't working, and I thoroughly enjoyed not working. I started, the first week after Jennie died, writing to her. I heard that that was good therapy, and you know, it really did help. So I wrote to her and I wrote poems about her, and somehow it seemed to bring her closer. Too, I started going to Compassionate Friends and that helped immeasurably. Just being around people who really understood people who really knew what it was like. I became acquainted with some really kind and caring people, people from all walks of life who shared a common thread that bound us together. I have never

252

been a 'clubby' sort of person, and I'd give anything if I was not eligible to join this one, but I must say, it helped.

There was a pretty Episcopal Church only a block away, and I started attending services there. Almost immediately I met some really lovely people, and I became very involved with the church. I was crazy about the Rector. He would talk to me about Jennie and make it seem like she was right there with us. He and his wife became very special friends to me. They even went with me to Compassionate Friends one time.

I also became re-acquainted with someone I had known when I lived in Wilmington before, and I met some, really, very interesting people through her. Soon I was meeting friends for lunch several times a week, and going up to the church to help cook for Mother Hubbard's cupboard at least once a week. To tell you the truth, I was going more than I wanted. And there was always this feeling of unreality, The REAL me was watching. Was this a dream? If it was, then WHEN was I going to wake up? Surely this was all a nightmare. This person couldn't be me. Jennie couldn't really be dead. God wouldn't do this to me. You, unless you've experienced it, can't understand. You KNOW it's true, but you can't believe it's true. Therefore, nothing seems real, who is this person that I've become? Yet, it happens to so many others. They had to take it, so I have to take it. There is nothing else you CAN do.

After I had been back in Wilmington for about a year, I decided I needed to go back to work. I had always enjoyed sales work. Beautiful clothes were always very important to me. There was an ad in the paper that Fleischman's Fine Clothiers needed a sales lady. This was a very nice, upscale store and I thought I'd probably enjoy working there. So I went to the store and applied for a part time position and got the job. Almost immediately I felt perfectly at home. This was a family owned and operated store, and I was very taken with every member of the family; I adore the grandchildren. I loved them all. I liked the others who worked there as well. The Fleischman's were very nice to me, and I will ever be grateful to them for helping me through a very sad period in my life. I worked at Fleischman's for ten long years. It is hard for me to comprehend that I was there so long. I'd probably still be working there, but about three years before I quit, I went with Kingsland to Virginia Beach to visit one of her daughters. While we were there we went to a store I'd never even heard about before. The name of the store was Stein Mart. I absolutely fell in love with this store. The clothes were beautiful and the prices were unbelievable! These were really nice clothes that I could afford. The people who worked there were lovely. Well, right then and there, I said, "If Stein Mart ever comes to Wilmington, then I certainly want to work there."

Three years later, miracle of miracles! Stein Mart came to Wilmington, and located only two blocks from where I live. I applied for a job, even before they opened and was hired for the Boutique. It was very hard to submit my letter of resignation to the Fleischman's, because, as I've said, I was really so fond of them, and they had, certainly, been nice to me. I still do and will always feel a kinship to them.

I started at Stein Mart the day they opened, and I have never regretted my decision to work there. I work much harder than I worked before; Stein Mart is a busy place, but I have never felt so completely that I was where I belonged to be. I love the other 'Boo' (Boutique) ladies, and they seem to like me just as well. But then, I like everybody in that store. Last year I was chosen to be 'Employee of the Year.' I was very proud of that. I tell our customers that I pay Stein Mart to let me work there. That is more truth than poetry, (as Mama would say) but our prices are so good that it is very hard to resist buying our clothes.

It has been almost 17 years now since Jennie left this world. I miss her constantly, but with the passing of time you get used to the pain. I'm not unhappy, actually I am quite content. I am surrounded by Jennie's pictures, I have one huge painting, and every time I look up, she is looking at me. Every night before I go to bed, and every time I go to work or go anywhere I tell her picture that I'll be with her when it's 'my time.' I truly believe I will. The night she died, (the first time) she awakened from a deep coma, and she started screaming, "No, no, no!" and then she started screaming, "Da, Da, Da! (That's what she called Daddy) I believe that he had come to get her, that she was saying, No, no, no! I took her little hand in mine and I said, "It's Mama, Jennie. I'm right here." Then she said, "MaMaMa" and that is when she drew her last breath.

So when it is my time, she'll be there to meet me. Daddy will be with her, I am sure, and Mama will be right there with them. And you know what I hope? I hope Bob will be there, too.

Maybe I'm just stupid, maybe he never loved me as much as I loved him, but for a little while, at least, I KNOW he loved me as much as he could love anybody.

As I have said before, I have lived many lives, many different kinds of lives. I doubt if anybody would want to trade lives with me, but you know what? I wouldn't trade my life for anybody else's either.

256

I wish I could go back and do it all over again. It would be so great to be "Little Billie Briar Hopper" again. I thought about calling this book 'Whatever Happened to Little Billie Briar Hopper?' But no, I'd go back further (or is it farther?) than that.

I'd like to go back to when.........

We moved to Littleton when I was six years old, my sister, King King was four and a half.........................

And

my name is

Willie Burton.

GREETINGS FROM WBT and "THE BRIARHOPPERS"
Left to right: Announcer Bill Bivens; Elmer; Billie; Mildred; Floyd; Bill Davis.
Back Row: Charlie; Gib; Roger; Claude Casey.

BECAUSE SHE'S GONE

It's almost Christmas time again

When love and peace and Joy all reign

A time when loved ones gather near

To share with us the Yule Tide Cheer.

But even in the midst of this

Inside we weep for those we miss

We long to see that face again

To hear her say, "I'm home again."

It's almost Christmas time again

But Christmas now is not the same

Nor will it ever be again

And joyous memories bring us pain

Because she's gone.

WE to ME

I was your shadow, but you were my light

Yours was the smile that made everything right

You were the baby I bounced on my knee

I still hear the echo of your baby glee.

The little girl who walked by my side

Little legs trying to match my stride

I was always so happy to have you near

I thanked God everyday for one so dear.

And before I knew it, what did I see?

A teenager you'd grown to be

And I turned around, and how could it be?

A beautiful woman was gazing at me.

Oh, yes, my darling, that was we

We, the way we used to be

And now is just so hard, you see

To face the fact, there's only me.

But time will pass, as time does do

And one day I'll be joining you

And never again, just me, but we

We'll joyfully share eternity.

I dedicate this, my book, to you, Jennie. I believe, I almost know, you helped me write it. I think you help me in many ways. You're looking after me now, as I looked after you, you're my guardian angel. I feel sometimes, that you are very near. Maybe this is why, although I am alone now, I don't feel alone. Maybe this is why I enjoy solitude, for in my solitude I feel very close to you.

All my love,

Mama Bill

262

2/08